Norm Foster

OFFICE HOURS

812.54
Fo 76
of

Playwrights Canada Press
Toronto • Canada

Office Hours © Copyright 1996 Norm Foster
Playwrights Canada Press
54 Wolseley St., 2nd fl. Toronto, Ontario CANADA M5T 1A5
Tel: (416) 703-0201 Fax: (416) 703-0059
e-mail: cdplays@interlog.com   http://www.puc.ca

Playwrights Canada Press publishes with the generous assistance of The Canada Council for the Arts - Writing and Publishing Section and the Ontario Arts Council.

Canadian Cataloguing in Publication Data
Foster, Norm, 1949 —
        Office hours

A play
ISBN 0-88754-541-6
I. Title.
PS8561.07745O33   1997   C812'.54   C97-932076-3
PR9199.3.F67O33   1997

First edition: May, 1998.
Printed and bound in Winnipeg, Manitoba, Canada.

Norm Foster and the "Popular" Label

Norm Foster, is generally recognized as Canada's most produced playwright, In a *Globe and Mail* article, Richard Ouzounian linked the Fredericton writer with Alan Ayckbourn, (England) and Neil Simon (United States) as the three most talked-about playwrights of their respective countries. Significantly, producers, especially of summer stock, now speak about "doing a Norm Foster" just as they talk about "doing a Neil Simon". Foster's humour does indeed contain echoes of the plot-driven comedies of Simon and Ayckbourn, but his writing also reflects the work of comic, character-driven playwrights such as Woody Allen and television comedians such as Jerry Seinfeld, combining the virtues of traditional stage plays with those of popular electronic culture.

Foster's path into comedy began with the roles of Elwood P. Dowd in "Harvey" and Jonathan Brewster in "Arsenic and Old Lace" while he worked as morning radio host in Fredericton in the early 1980's. In 1981, Theatre Fredericton produced his first script, "Friends and Family" (unpublished), with a plot not too far removed in comic structure from those plays in which he had acted. This early work attracted the attention of Theatre New Brunswick's Artistic Director, Malcolm Black, who, in 1983 and 1984, mounted the first professional productions of Foster's "Sinners", and "The Melville Boys". In the years following, TNB introduced "My Darling Judith" (1987), "The Affections of May" (1990), "The Motor Trade" (1991), "Wrong for Each Other" (1992), and "Office Hours" (1996). In fifteen years, the prolific Foster, who continues to host a morning radio show, has had a number of plays open on other stages around the country: "Windfall" (1985), "Bravado" (1988), "Opening Night" (1989), "The Sitter" (1992), "Ned Durango Comes to Big Oak" (1994), "Jupiter in July" (1997), and "The Last Resort" (1997). Acting alongside his wife, Janet Monid, Foster has launched "The Long Weekend" (1994), "Ned Durango Comes to Big Oak" (1995), and "Here on the Flight Path" (1997) as dinner theatre productions.

Professional and amateur directors find in Foster's scripts a number of attractions. For the strictly bottom-line, show-me-the-money, fiscally challenged producer, these scripts have a two-edged appeal: small casts and, generally, one set. For the audience, the emotional fragility of

Foster's characters and the immediacy of his plots have the familiar fluency of the best of the television comedies. This ready accessibility, along with themes which focus on the complexities of daily survival and a comic turn of phrase which enhances the fast pace of his narratives, are key to Foster's popularity (as, indeed, they are to Simon's and Seinfeld's).

While he has traditionally worked within the full-length play structure, Foster has recently experimented with shorter narratives. "The Sitter" (1992), untypical in that it focuses more on its developing story line than on comic repartee between characters, was his first one-act play. "Here on the Flight Path" (1997) follows a not-overly-ambitious writer through three one-act relationships which come his way on adjoining balconies as the flat next door is rented by a succession of young women. "Office Hours", in two acts, has six separate individually titled segments which, through a series of workshops, evolved into a single, multi-linked play. At the centre of the play's appeal is the audience's shared awareness of knowing more about the characters than those individuals are willing to admit to themselves: the 200-pound jockey who is deep in denial of the weighty obvious; the totally domineering mother who refuses to believe she has an authoritarian bone in her body; the insecure movie producer who won't acknowledge the antecedents of an "original" script concerning a young English plane-crash survivor named Trevor who is raised by African apes to become lord of the jungle; and various other characters, all obsessed with holding their lives together by keeping reality at bay.

The worlds of denial are surrounded by engaging theatrical contexts. For instance, "The Dismissal" builds a clever parody of Arthur Miller's office scene in which Howard dismisses Willy Loman. Artie points out that "promises had been made" — eternal friendship, and a job — by Stan's father across the very desk where now Stan, the late racetrack owner's son, is faced with the unpleasant necessity of banning corpulent Artie from the backs of long-suffering horses. Artie hasn't been a winner in years. Business is business. ("Everybody's gotta pull his own weight", Howard tells Willy.) The truths which gradually unfold destroy both Artie's sense of personal worth and the warm memories of his self-constructed past. Continuing this theme, in "The Analyst", the suicidal Neil's repetition of Willy's famous cry "I am not a dime a dozen!" completes the subtle homage to the American playwright.

Four centuries ago the distinction between academic and popular theatre gave Philip Sydney a stick with which to beat the creative upstarts of the popular Elizabethan stage — Marlowe, Kyd, Shakespeare

— who were muscling in on the University Wits, now deservedly forgotten. Today this distinction gives Canadian funding agencies a stick with which to keep popular, though academically less significant, productions at a distance. (Foster's plays are "Canadian" but that label doesn't shake The Canada Council's money tree as it did in the dear dead days of the Gaspé Manifesto.) The result has been that the popular appeal of Foster's plays is both the obstacle and key to his success.

The "popular" label also allows academics to avoid playwrights such as Norm Foster almost entirely. Purveyors of Canadian 'canonicity' turn for support to the anthologized scripts published in volumes edited by professors. Explorations of Canadian scripts in our theatrical periodicals, such as *Theatre Research in Canada* and *Canadian Drama* (now defunct), usually focus on texts which lend themselves to such modern critical frameworks as the post-structural, deconstructionist, semiotic, phenomenological, psychoanalytical, Marxist, Feminist, Feminist-Marxist, and so on. Popular activities which are difficult to gather under one or more of these theoretical umbrellas are either redefined in terms which bring them within the academic franchises (*viz.* circuses, political revolutions, religious orations, polemics on or by the politically correct) or else they are ignored by academics for whom 'popularity' has not been a useful critical tool. This lack of academic involvement with Foster's work has had a measurable affect on his position in Canadian theatre.

Foster stands as English Canada's premiere comic playwright. His popular comedy succeeds because, like Simon and Allen's, it places before us the neuroses, psychoses and repressions which link the comic to the tragic. Its immediacy sidesteps academic discourses which destroy through dissection. It holds a mirror up to the shared foible of its audience. It first invokes laughter. Then recognition. Then it makes us a little more accepting of what it means to be human.

Edward Mullally
University of New Brunswick
September 1997

CHARACTERS

THE REPORTER

Warren Kimble	A television news reporter
Pam Gerard	A television news producer
One-armed Man	A viewer

THE PITCH

Gordon Blaine	A Canadian film producer
Francine Majors	A Canadian film producer
Bobby Holland	An American film director

THE AGENT

Mark Young	An agent
Ellie Young	Mark's wife

THE VISIT

Richard Penny	A lawyer
Rhonda Penny	Richard's mother
Lloyd Penny	Richard's father

THE DISMISSAL

Stan Thurber	A racetrack owner
Artie Barnes	A racetrack employee

THE ANALYST

Sharon Freeman	A psychiatrist
Man	A patient
Neil Penny	A patient
Rhonda Penny	Neil's Mother
Lloyd Penny	Neil's Father
Artie Barnes	A patient

Author's note: The play can be done with as few as five or as many as seventeen actors. The author suggests that six actors would sustain the flow and separation nicely.

Running time: Approximately 2 hours with intermission.

Role Breakdown for a Cast of 5

Actor #1	Warren Kimble, Mark Young, Artie Barnes, Neil Penny
Actress #1	Pam Gerard, Ellie Young, Sharon Freeman
Actor #2	One-armed Man, Bobby Holland, Lloyd Penny
Actress #2	Francine Majors, Rhonda Penny
Actor #3	Gordon Blaine, Richard Penny, Stan Thurber, Man

"Office Hours" premiered at Theatre New Brunswick, Fredericton, NB, October 11 - November 2, 1996, with the following cast and crew:

WARREN/MARK/ARTIE/NEIL	*Frank McAnulty*
PAM/ELLIE/SHARON/	*Elizabeth Goodyear*
ONE-ARMED MAN/BOBBY/LLOYD	*David Hughes*
GORDON/RICHARD/STANAN/MAN	*David Nairn*
FRANCINE/RHONDA	*Nonnie Griffin*

Directed by Ted Follows.
Stage Manager - Henry Bertrand.
Set design by David Westlake.
Lighting by Tim Gorman.

The Reporter

Time: The present.

Place: The office of television news producer Pan Gerard.

The office in each of the following pieces is quite nicely furnished, but not to excess. In the office is a desk and chair (left), for the office occupant, a couple of chairs for visitors, plus a couch, in the corner (u.r.) there is a coat rack on which hangs a trenchcoat. There is also a cabinet in which there is a bar, two or three plants round out the decor. As the scene opens, we see WARREN KIMBLE pacing in the office. WARREN wears a rumpled, well-worn suit, with a dark sweater vest underneath. He is talking to himself, rehearsing for a future conversation.

WARREN

You twit. You inarticulate, BMW-driving, tofu-eating twit. (*beat*) No, that might be too confrontational. Uh ... All right, let's try this. You know something, Ms. Gerard? Mrs. Gerard? Pam? Can I call you Pam, Pam? No, the more I say it, the more it sounds like Spam. Pamela, I'm given to understand that you don't like my work. No, too civil. Be a little more intimidating. Give it the Robert DeNiro inflection. You got a problem with my work? Are you serious? You can't be serious. My work? Are you tellin' me you got a problem with my work? No. Okay, start off with a joke. All right. All right. Pam, don't you think it's funny that my name is Warren Kimble and yours is Pam Gerard? Huh? Kimble, Gerard? We've got kind of a "Fugitive" thing happening here. Kind of a David Janssen, Barry Morse kind of thing. No, screw the jokes. Get right to the point Pam, I get the feeling that you don't like my work. Well, right now, honey, I don't like my work either. And I'll tell you why. I'm news reporter, Pam. I've been working my way up for twenty-three years. That's right. Some of us work our way up. We don't marry the station manager and go from television bingo hostess to news producer just like that. But, that doesn't bother me. No, that doesn't bother me one goddamned bit. What bothers me is that I was the top reporter in this city at one time, I did stories with integrity. Stories I was proud of. And now? Two weeks ago I covered a wake for a racehorse. What the hell is that?! So the horse died. Who gives a shit? It's not Black Beauty for Godssake. And last week you sent me to interview that Pentecostal group that wants to put a loin cloth on the statue of Cupid. So, there I am interviewing the queen of the tight-asses while Cupid urinates into a fountain behind me. How in the hell am I supposed to do good work in a situation like that, you slack-jawed, addle-brained, Melrose Place-watching, harpy. I need the hard-hitting stories. And I'm not talking about doing "Death Of A Salesman" every night. Just something newsworthy. That's all I ask. I mean, hell, I'm forty-eight years old. I've got a mortgage I'm paying off and a kid I'm trying to put through university. That's a school, Pam. A big one with people your age in it — but, I'd sooner be out of work than do the crap stories you're giving me. So, that's it. That's all I have to say. And if you want to fire me, you go right the hell ahead because, quite frankly, lady, I don't give a tinker's toot. Oh, and one more thing. I don't appreciate being summoned into your office like one of your underlings and then being left here to ponder my fate while you get called away on some petty emergency. You understand what I'm saying, you scrotum-cracking, Alanis Morrisette-loving, preening little tart! Warren Kimble waits for no one!

> *The door opens and PAM GERARD enters. She is dressed in business clothes, and she carries a binder and a paperback book.*

PAM   Sorry to keep you waiting.

WARREN   Oh, that's okay. I don't mind waiting. I just made
              myself at home. Beautiful office by the way, Pam.

                        PAM throws WARREN a cautioning look.

              Pamela.

                        PAM is still staring him down.

              Ms. Gerard.

PAM   It'll do I suppose.

                        *PAM moves to the chair behind her desk. She
                        puts the binder down and arranges some
                        papers.*

WARREN   *Beat* Sounded like something big.

PAM   What?

WARREN   When you got called away there. It sounded big.

PAM   Oh, I just had to find a crew to cover a jumper down
              on Kensington. No big deal.

WARREN   A jumper?

PAM   Yeah, some nut on a ledge.

WARREN   I talked a jumper down once you know.

PAM   (*not interested*) Really?

WARREN   Yeah, about five years ago. This guy was on a bridge
              and we heard the police call ....

PAM   *Beat* Warren, let's get down to business shall we?

WARREN   Hmm?

PAM   Business? Our meeting?

WARREN	Oh. Right. Right. (*noticing the paperback, he picks it up*) Oooh, Margaux Kenyon, huh? Pretty steamy stuff. I read her last one, *Spellbound In Spandex*.. I'll tell you, she cooks with gas.
PAM	Warren?
WARREN	Oh, that's a nice week-at-a-glance. Very nice. Is that leather bound?
PAM	Yes.
WARREN	Very handsome. Where'd you get it?
PAM	Some obnoxious salesman came in last week and I bought it just to get rid of him.
WARREN	I've been looking for something like this.
PAM	Warren, I don't like your work.
WARREN	(*beat*) What?
PAM	I don't like your work.
WARREN	I'm sorry. My work?
PAM	Yes, Warren, your work. That thing we pay you for.
WARREN	Uh-huh. Uh-huh. Well, I must say this comes as a complete surprise.
PAM	It does?
WARREN	Right out of left field. I had no idea.
PAM	Well, I'm sorry, Warren, but I like to lay my cards on the table.
WARREN	I see that. (*beat*) Have you ever noticed that your name is Gerard and mine is Kimble? You know what that's like? That's like the ... uh ... the uh...
PAM	The what?

WARREN   You know. The ... uh ... the running guy. You know? He killed his wife, but he didn't do it. Somebody else did it. And then there's a train crash, and now he's running. Always running.

PAM *Beat*   So, what do you think about what I just said, Warren?

WARREN   Uh ... what you just said? Well, Pam, Ms. Gerard, I think we should talk about it, Sure. See where you think my strengths lie, where my weaknesses are. What needs to be fine-tuned. You know, do a little tweaking.

PAM   No, I don't want to tweak, Warren. No tweaking. No fine-tuning. I want to fire you.

WARREN   Fire me?

PAM   Yes.

WARREN   Well ... I, uh...

PAM   Unfortunately my husband likes you.

WARREN   He does?

PAM   Yes.

WARREN   Your husband the station manager?

PAM   No, my husband the Zulu warrior. Yes, my husband the station manager. He thinks you lend experience to the news. A little seasoning, as he puts it.

WARREN   Seasoning?

PAM   Yes.

WARREN   (*humbly*) Well.

PAM   He particularly liked that Cupid story you did last week.

WARREN   Did he? Well, you know, I was pleased with that story myself. In fact.

PAM   But, I disagree with my husband. I don't think you lend experience to the news at all. I think you lend age to it. You're the oldest on-air person we have, Warren.

WARREN   Oh, no, I don't think so.

PAM   You are. I checked.

WARREN   No, I think Daphne Hilyard is older than I am.

PAM   She's forty-three.

WARREN   She's what? Is that what she told you?

PAM   She's forty-three, Warren. And she does a gardening show. The viewers don't mind hearing about gardens from middle-aged people. Gardening and cooking. That's where the middle-aged broadcaster is going.

WARREN   I don't cook. I've got a bit of a green thumb though.

PAM   I don't care about your green thumb, Warren. You can have a purple ass for all I care. You're not getting a gardening show or a cooking show.

WARREN   So, what am I going to be doing?

PAM   The desk.

WARREN   What?

PAM   I'm putting you on the desk. I want you to write up stories for the six and the eleven, but as far as on-camera work goes, I want to limit it.

WARREN   Limit it?

PAM   Yes.

WARREN   To what?

PAM
To the occasional special interest story. Like that horse wake thing you did. Stories like that.

WARREN
I see. Well, you know, those kinds of stories are fine, Spam. Pam! Ms. Gerard, But I was hoping for something more substantial. Something I could really sink my reporter's teeth into.

PAM
I'm sorry, Warren, but I'm going for a more contemporary look on the news hour and you don't fit that look. Now, if you don't think you can handle the desk, you're certainly free to turn it down.

WARREN
And what if I do ... turn it down?

PAM
Well, my husband asked me to find a place for you and I did. If you turn it down and decide to move on, well, that's up to you. So, is that what you're doing?

WARREN
What?

PAM
Are you turning it down? Because if you are, then I've got to find someone to replace you, and I'd like to get on it right away.

WARREN
Uh ... no. No, I can do the desk thing, I mean, writing has always been my strong suit anyway. So, yeah. Yeah. I can do that.

PAM
(*picks up the phone and presses two digits*) All right. It's settled then.

WARREN
When does the change take effect?

PAM
Right now.

WARREN
Now? Today? Boy, that's kind of fast, don't you think? I mean...

PAM
(*into phone*) Dave? Pam. I'm sending Warren Kimble down to you. Give him some copy to work on for the six, would you please? ... That's right, Warren Kimble ... Dave, just do it, would you, please? Thank you. (*hangs up*) There. That's that.

WARREN   Right.

PAM   Oh, and there'll be a slight pay adjustment as well because of the reassignment.

WARREN   Pay adjustment?

PAM   Yes, the new position has a lower profile, less responsibility...

The phone on PAM's desk rings.

Excuse me. (*answering*) Pam Gerard ... Yeah? ... Oh, what the hell ... (*checks her watch*) All right, it's four fifteen now. If nothing's happened by five, come on in .... Right ... (*she hangs up*) Now we've got two jumpers, out there, and what do you wanna bet they don't make a move in time for the six clock? We're done here, right?

WARREN   Yeah. Yeah.

PAM   Good. Well, things to do. Excuse me.

PAM exits, WARREN stands there for a moment.

WARREN   The desk? Writing copy? I don't think so, Missy. No, I don't think so. And I'm gonna tell her that too. She likes cards on the table? She'll get cards on the table.

The door opens and PAM enters again. She breezes by WARREN to her desk.

PAM   You're still here.

WARREN   Just leaving.

PAM grabs her binder off her desk.

PAM   (*moving back to the door*) Was there something else?

WARREN   No. Nothing.

PAM	You're sure?
WARREN	Absolutely.
PAM	Well, let's get back to work then.
WARREN	You bet. You bet.

> *PAM exits. WARREN moves to the door. he closes the door softly.*

(*to himself again*) Back to work, huh? You don't know the meaning of work, you spoon-fed, cell phone-worshipping, flavoured coffee-drinking miscreant. I should be the one in charge here. That's right. I was the next in line when Roberts moved on, but your husband promoted you instead. Oh that was a slap in the face. I'll tell you this much though, the first time you screw up, sweetheart, this job is mine and you know it. Well, you said it yourself: He likes my work. Of course he does. What's not to like? No. I'll just bide my time. And you keep looking over your shoulder, Pam, because every time you do, I'll be there like a festering sore. That's me, baby. A festering sore.

> *The door opens and a ONE-ARMED MAN enters the office. He is wearing jeans and a windbreaker.*

MAN	Are you the producer here?
WARREN	What?
MAN	The producer? Are you him?
WARREN	You've only got one arm.
MAN	What?
WARREN	You're a one-armed man.
MAN	I asked you if you're the producer.

WARREN   Hmm? Oh, well, I should be. I've worked hard enough
                for it.

                    The MAN pulls a knife out of his jacket.

                Whoa! What the hell is that?

MAN   You ruined my life.

WARREN   I what?

MAN   You ruined my life!

WARREN   No, you've got the wrong guy. You must have.

MAN   Your people shot some film of me and my girlfriend at
                a sidewalk cafe. Do you remember that?

WARREN   Sidewalk cafe? Uh...

MAN   My girlfriend and I were kissing. Your station was
                doing a story on public displays of affection and how
                they're a sure sign of Spring.

WARREN   Sounds like us. So?

MAN   So, when you ran the story you put a graphic on the
                screen that identified me as that mass murderer Charles
                Lester.

WARREN   Oh, my God. You're Charles Lester?

MAN   No, you idiot! You got the graphics from two different
                stories mixed up. Under Lester's picture it said "All
                You Need Is Love".

WARREN   Oops.

MAN   Yeah, so now, everywhere I go, people think I'm
                Charles Lester. I got fired from my job, and my wife
                left me.

WARREN   Well you're wife must know you're not Charles Les ....
                Oh, the girlfriend.

MAN   Right. So, that's why I'm here. To finish off the person responsible.

WARREN   (*beat*) All right, let me take you to her. (*he starts to move*)

MAN   Stay there!

WARREN   But, I'm not the producer!

MAN   Not the producer, my ass. This is the producer's office, isn't it? That's what it says on the door.

WARREN   Yes, it is, but....

MAN   And you're the senior person here, at least from what I can see.

WARREN   Actually, there's a woman who does the gardening show who I'm sure is older. She says she's forty-three but...

MAN   Never mind! (*moving toward WARREN*)

WARREN   Oh, now, wait a minute, wait a minute. Hurting me, what's that gonna get you?

MAN   Satisfaction.

WARREN   No, that won't get you satisfaction. They'll put you away. You'll lose everything.

MAN   I've already lost everything.

WARREN   Oh, come on, you must have something going for you. You ... you've got your health.

They both look at his missing arm.

You've got your girlfriend.

MAN   She left me.

WARREN   Oh.

MAN   For your cameraman.

WARREN   Well, lemme take you to him then. Which one was it? Lenny? Short guy? I hate that son of a bitch.

MAN   I don't want him. I want you. The person in charge.

WARREN   I'm not in charge.

MAN   Go to hell.

WARREN   I'm not! You obviously know nothing about the news business, do you? You see, all the producing jobs and on-air jobs are filled by women these days. It's a cosmetic business. It's not how well you inform the public anymore, it's how well you look while you misinform them. Now, the woman you're after is Pam Gerard, and she's right out here somewhere.

> *WARREN moves toward the door, but the MAN steps in his way and WARREN runs into the knife. WARREN grabs his stomach and steps back in disbelief.*

What are you ... You ... You stabbed me.

MAN   Oops.

> *WARREN falls to his knees. the ONE-ARMED MAN runs out of the office.*

WARREN   Wait ... Oh, my God ... Oh, God. (*he makes it to the couch and sits*) Help! Anybody! God, I hope it wasn't a dirty knife. (*looks at the phone on PAM's desk*) 911. Gotta call 911. (*he moves to the desk and sits in PAM's chair*)

> *PAM GERARD enters the office.*

PAM   Warren?

WARREN   Oh, thank God.

PAM   What are you doing in my chair?

WARREN	I can explain that. (*he struggles to remove himself from the chair*)
PAM	I certainly hope you can.
WARREN	I'm ... I've been stabbed.
PAM	What? (*sees the wound*) Oh, my God. Stabbed? What happened?
WARREN	911...
PAM	What?
WARREN	Call 911.
PAM	Oh, 911! Right. 911. (*dialing the phone*)
WARREN	A man with one arm. He thought I was you.
PAM	A what? A man with one arm?
WARREN	You got his graphics mixed up.
PAM	(*into phone*) Yes, I need an ambulance at the CKG Television studios. A man's been stabbed ... Yes .... No, he's still conscious ... All right, thank you. (*she hangs up*) They're on their way, Warren. How are you feeling? (*she punches two digits on the phone*)
WARREN	Weak. I think I'm going into shock.
PAM	Well, hold on. They'll be here any minute. A one-armed man? You mean like in "The Fugitive"?
WARREN	That's it!! That's it!!
PAM	(*into phone*) Sally, get into my office right away. And bring a cameraman. Lenny if you can find him. (*hangs up*)
WARREN	What are you doing?
PAM	I'm getting Sally Fong in here.

WARREN   What for?

PAM   To cover the story.

WARREN   Sally Fong?

PAM   Yes. I mean, how often does something like this fall into our laps?

WARREN   Sally Fong?

PAM   Yes. Boy, the blood doesn't show up very well on that dark sweater, does it?

WARREN   What about me? Why can't I cover the story?

PAM   What? No, you can't cover the story. You're on the desk now. Can you take that sweater off?

WARREN   What?

PAM   The sweater. Let's take it off.

> *WARREN takes his jacket off, then his sweater. PAM joins in, helping him pull it over his head.*

WARREN   Pam, please, I want this story. This is Pulitzer Prize material.

PAM   Warren, didn't we just have a little talk about this very thing? Hmm? And didn't we agree that we were going to limit your on camera appearances to a certain type of story? Well, this is not one of those stories.

WARREN   But, I can do this...

PAM   Warren, please, don't ask me again. I've already had enough hassles for one day, what with those bloody jumpers not being able to make up their minds. Where the hell is she? Sally?! (*she exits*)

WARREN   Wait! Wait... (*he collapses behind the desk*) You untutored, outfit-wearing, light beer-drinking...

PAM enters the office.

PAM   Did you say something?

WARREN   Nothing. Nothing.

PAM exits.

... petrified piece of pig dung.

He collapses on the desk. Lights down.

End.

The Pitch

Time: The present.

*Place: The office of film producer GORDON
BLAINE.*

*As the scene opens, GORDON BLAINE and
FRANCINE MAJORS are on stage.
GORDON paces. FRANCINE sits on the
couch.*

GORDON It's three forty-five. Who does he think he is, keeping
us waiting like this?

FRANCINE Now, Gordon, he's only fifteen minutes late. Are you
sure he said three-thirty?

GORDON Yes, I wrote it down in my week-at-a-glance. See?
(*pointing to his week-at-a-glance*)

FRANCINE Oh, that's new.

GORDON Hmm?

FRANCINE The week-at-a-glance.

GORDON Oh, yeah, I bought it the other day from some pushy
salesman. Wouldn't take no for an answer.

FRANCINE Nice.

GORDON Who the hell does he think he is?

FRANCINE Maybe he got lost. I mean, he's new to the city. We
should've sent a car for him.

GORDON No. No, that would make us look too anxious. Too
accommodating.

FRANCINE   I think it would have been the courteous thing to do.

GORDON   No. He would've mistaken it for sucking up. I mean, he's probably got producers grovelling at his feet constantly. I want us to be different. I want him to notice us.

FRANCINE   By being rude? I don't think we have to be rude.

GORDON   We're not being rude. We're just laying the ground rules. We're letting him know there's going to be no sucking up here. You got in touch with our lawyer, right?

FRANCINE   He's on alert. If we agree to something in principle today he'll be ready to draw up an agreement.

GORDON   Good. Is he gay?

FRANCINE   Who? Our lawyer?

GORDON   I think he's gay.

FRANCINE   I don't know.

GORDON   I mean, I don't care if he's gay. What do I care if he's gay? I don't. I'm just curious.

FRANCINE   Well, I couldn't tell you.

GORDON   His office is very neat though, don't you think? Very tidy.

FRANCINE   I hadn't noticed.

GORDON   Very tidy. Boy, "Philadelphia" was a great movie, wasn't it? Now, there was a movie.

There is a knock at the door.

Well, it's about bloody time. Are you ready?

FRANCINE   Yes. All set. (*she stands and moves to the centre of the office*)

GORDON   Remember. No sucking up.

FRANCINE   Right.

GORDON   Just be cavalier.

FRANCINE   Cavalier.

GORDON   Nonchalant even.

FRANCINE   Got it.

GORDON   You don't care about him one way or the other.

FRANCINE   Why don't I just knee him in the groin? Is that what you want?

GORDON   All right, here we go.

>*GORDON opens the door. BOBBY*
>*HOLLAND stands there.*

Bobby Holland! Bobby! Bobby! Come in, please, come in.

BOBBY   Thank you.

>*BOBBY enters the office.*

GORDON   So good to see you. So very nice. I'm Gordon Blaine, and this is my co-producer, Francine Majors.

>*They all shake hands.*

FRANCINE   Hello.

BOBBY   Hi. Sorry I'm late.

GORDON   Late? Are you late? I didn't notice.

BOBBY   Yes, I got lost.

GORDON   You what?

BOBBY   I got lost.

GORDON   Oh, no.

FRANCINE   Ohhh.

GORDON   Are you serious?

BOBBY   Well, the cabbie wasn't sure where the place was, and then traffic was tied up because of a guy on a ledge down the street.

GORDON   A what?

BOBBY   Yeah, there's some nut on a ledge threatening to jump.

GORDON   This close to rush hour? Some people have no consideration.

BOBBY   Well, I'm here now, so...

GORDON   I can't believe this. (*to FRANCINE*) I knew we should've sent a car.

BOBBY   No, that's okay.

GORDON   No, you're new in town. (*to FRANCINE*) We should've sent a car.

FRANCINE   Well, we'll know better next time.

GORDON   That's right. We certainly will. Live and learn. We're very sorry, Bobby. This is extremely embarrassing.

BOBBY   It's nothing, really.

GORDON   Can you forgive us?

BOBBY   It's nothing.

GORDON   Well, have a seat, please. Make yourself comfortable.

BOBBY   Thank you. (*he sits*)

GORDON   (*to FRANCINE*) Next time we send a car. (*to BOBBY*)
          Can I get you a drink, Bobby? Scotch, vodka, rum?

BOBBY   A scotch would be fine, thank you.

GORDON   Scotch it is.

BOBBY   Straight up, please.

GORDON   You bet. (*he moving to get the drink*)

BOBBY   A double, if that's all right.

GORDON   Of course it's all right. (*to FRANCINE*) You see that?
          Now, that's a director. Double scotch straight up.
          Huh? Not like these young pantywaists coming up
          today, drinking their wine coolers and their spritzers.
          Do you think John Huston would drink a spritzer?
          John Huston would spit on a spritzer!

FRANCINE Well, this is really a treat, Bobby. I'm a very big fan.
          We both are.

GORDON   We're huge fans.

BOBBY   Well, thank you. You're very kind.

GORDON   Yes, what an honour. You know I can't tell you how
          surprised I was when you called me last week and said
          you wanted to come up here and pitch a movie idea to
          us.

FRANCINE He was beside himself.

GORDON   I was more than beside myself. I was encircling
          myself. I mean, Bobby Holland, the most successful
          director in Hollywood over the past twenty-five years.
          Well, your very first movie, "Cold Steel", grossed
          over twenty million, right?

BOBBY   Right.

GORDON	And then there was "Footsteps in the Alley", about organized crime infiltrating professional bowling. God, I loved that one. And the casting was inspired. I mean, who knew that Sean Connery could bowl? And that one pulled in over, what, sixty million?
BOBBY	About that.
GORDON	Sixty mil. I'm getting a cramp just thinking about it.
BOBBY	Well, I've been pretty lucky.
GORDON	Lucky, hell! You haven't had one flop. That's a remarkable record. That's why I couldn't believe it when you called. Not that we're not capable of producing good work, Frannie and me. We've produced some films we're very proud of, haven't we Frannie?
FRANCINE	Extremely proud.
GORDON	Extremely. And you know, right now we're very close to securing the movie rights to Margaux Kenyon's new book. Isn't that right, Fran?
FRANCINE	Very close.
BOBBY	(*impressed*) Margaux Kenyon?
GORDON	That's right. Got a big meeting with her agent on Monday. Disney's after it too, but I don't think it's Disney's style. Disney doesn't do sex very well. Dogs and cats finding their way home: they do great. Sex, I don't think so.
BOBBY	Well, I hope it works out for you.
GORDON	Thank you. So, we are making a name for ourselves. In fact, CKG, one of the local TV stations, did a feature on us last month. What did they call us, Frannie?
FRANCINE	A couple of plucky producers.

GORDON	Plucky producers. It was a shlocky piece but it gets our names out there, right?
BOBBY	That's right, That's very important.
FRANCINE	So, tell me, Bobby, why come to Canada?
BOBBY	Well...
GORDON	Yes, I mean, a man of your immense talent must have producers in the States just wetting themselves to produce one of your movies?
BOBBY	Well, Gordon ... Can I call you Gordon?
GORDON	Hey, call me whatever you like. Call me Ismail for Godssake.
BOBBY	Well, the truth is Gordon, I don't like what's happening down there right now, it seems that all they're worried about these days is how much money the film will make.
GORDON	The bastards. I hate that.
BOBBY	You see, the problem is, they lack vision.
GORDON	Hey, you want vision? We've got vision. Superman doesn't have as much vision.
BOBBY	Well, that's what I was hoping.
FRANCINE	Excuse me. I know this may be inappropriate to bring up at this point, Bobby, but the buzz around the industry is that ... well, that you've run out of ideas.
GORDON	You're right. That's very inappropriate.
BOBBY	No, let her talk. Please. Go on, Francine.
FRANCINE	Well, I mean, you haven't made a movie in almost four years now, and I've asked around and, well, the talk is that the idea well has dried up. I'm sorry, but that's what I hear.

BOBBY	No, don't be sorry. I've heard the talk too. But no, that's not why I haven't made a movie in so long.
GORDON	Of course it's not.
BOBBY	I just haven't been able to find a producer that I have faith in.
GORDON	That's all it is.
BOBBY	It seems like nobody cares about the quality of the product anymore.
GORDON	It sickens me to hear that, Bobby. Sickens me. Why, you're a giant in the industry. You should be given carte blanche to make whatever kind of movie you want. Quality or not.
BOBBY	Well, I appreciate that, Gordon.
GORDON	It comes from the heart.
FRANCINE	So, the idea well isn't dry?
GORDON	Francine, please..
BOBBY	It's okay, Gordon. Francine has every right to ask these questions. I mean, if all goes well, you two are going to be sinking a lot of money into this project. And I won't lie to you, I don't make cheap movies.
GORDON	And dammit, we don't want you to. Now, tell us about this new idea you have,
BOBBY	Well, Gordon, Francine, it's something I'm very excited about. Very excited. Mind you, it's not "Death of a Salesman".
GORDON	What is?
BOBBY	But it has substance and it has meaning, and I think I can get Charlie Sheen.

> *BOBBY gets up and pours himself another
> drink. He leaves the bottle on the desk.*

GORDON   Charlie Sheen?

BOBBY   Charlie Sheen.

GORDON   Get out of here.

BOBBY   He owes me one.

GORDON   Charlie Sheen? Did you hear that, Frannie?

BOBBY   And if not Charlie then one of the Baldwins for sure.

GORDON   The Baldwins. Oh, they're very hot. Very hot. Which one?

BOBBY   Alec, maybe.

GORDON   Oooh, Alec.

BOBBY   Maybe Billy.

GORDON   Billy is good.

BOBBY   Daniel for sure.

GORDON   Who cares? They all look the same anyway. We'll get Daniel. We'll bill him as Alec.

BOBBY   All right, here it is. Let's start from the opening shot.

GORDON   Opening shot.

BOBBY   It's an aerial view of nothing but trees.

GORDON   Trees. Environment. Good.

BOBBY   Now, as we fly over these trees we see smoke coming from what appears to be wreckage down below.

GORDON   Oh-oh.

BOBBY	So, we move in closer, zooming in through the billowing smoke, zooming zooming, smoke flying past, wondering what we're going to find, wondering, zooming, wondering, zooming, and then, suddenly, we see it! It's the wreckage of a small plane. Bang! Opening credits.
GORDON	Whew! I might need a minute to catch my breath.
BOBBY	Now there is only one survivor of this plane crash, and it's a small boy, about one, maybe two years old. His parents both have perished — we find out when we see their wedding picture smoldering in the ruins.
FRANCINE	How do we know they're dead from the picture?
BOBBY	Through symbolism, the picture bursts into flames.
GORDON	Oh, like that map at the beginning of "Bonanza".
BOBBY	Right. Now, the child is all alone and, as it turns out, the plane has crashed on an escarpment in the jungles of Africa.
GORDON	Oh, my God.
FRANCINE	An escarpment?
BOBBY	That's right.
FRANCINE	In Africa?
BOBBY	Yes. And there isn't a human being within a hundred mile radius.
GORDON	Well, how does the kid survive?
BOBBY	Well, now, this is where it takes a crazy kind of a turn.
GORDON	A twist. I like it. Twists are very big these days.
BOBBY	Now, you're going to have to be very open-minded here. Can you do that?

GORDON   I'm open.

BOBBY   You're open?

GORDON   Twenty-four hours. I never close.

BOBBY   All right, Here it is. (*beat*) The boy is raised by apes.
                (*BOBBY pours himself another drink*)

FRANCINE   (*beat*) Apes?

GORDON   Apes?

BOBBY   Apes.

GORDON   (*beat*) Okay, okay, I can see that. The apes treat him
                like one of their own.

BOBBY   Exactly.

GORDON   I can see that.

FRANCINE   Excuse me, but, isn't that like...

GORDON   Francine please. Let him finish. Go on, Bobby. Go
                on.

BOBBY   Okay, so this boy is raised by this colony of apes and
                he grows up there in the jungle not even knowing that
                an outside world exists.

GORDON   Does he have a name? What do we call this kid?

BOBBY   Oh, he's got a name, sure. Trevor.

FRANCINE   Trevor?

BOBBY   Trevor.

GORDON   Well, how does he get Trevor? Is that his real name?

BOBBY   No, of course not. How would the apes know his real
                name? He was too young to tell them, right?

GORDON Oh, right. So, how does he get Trevor?

BOBBY Well that's the irony, you see, Trevor is actually his father's name and the apes find his father's passport in the wreckage and they think it's the kid's.

FRANCINE (*beat*) So, they get the name Trevor off the father's passport?

BOBBY Right.

GORDON Ah-hahhh.

FRANCINE Now, wait a minute...

BOBBY No, please. I don't want to lose my train of thought. So, Trevor grows up among the apes and pretty soon, because of his ability to reason, he becomes the master of all of the animals. Kind of the duke of the jungle ... or the lord. I haven't decided yet. And he communicates with them. They seem to understand what he's saying, even though to us, it's gibberish.

GORDON Okay, okay, now here's where I start to get worried because, and I don't want to be a naysayer, Bobby, believe me. That's the last thing I wanna be, but this is starting to sound a little derivative in parts.

BOBBY Derivative how?

GORDON Well, it's starting to sound a little bit like that Rex Harrison "Doctor Doolittle" thing. You know, talking to the animals.

BOBBY No, not at all.

GORDON You don't think so?

BOBBY No, those animals weren't real animals, Doolittle was talking to two-headed llamas.

GORDON Okay.

BOBBY This is real. Very real.

GORDON   Absolutely. Just playing devil's advocate. Please, go on.

FRANCINE   Gordon? Doesn't this sound like...

GORDON   Francine, the man is speaking. Please.

BOBBY   Okay. Now, Trevor becomes a true friend to these jungle animals, you know, giving them a boost up to eat from the higher branches, straightening up their caves for them. But, he develops a closer, more special relationship with one animal in particular. (*moving to pour himself another drink*)

FRANCINE   (*picking up the bottle*) Let me guess. A chimpanzee.

BOBBY   No, it's not a chimpanzee.

            BOBBY goes to the cabinet and takes out another bottle, he opens it and carries it with him.

GORDON   Of course, it's not a chimpanzee. What kind of an idea is that? It's been done to death.

FRANCINE   Gordon, can't you see...

GORDON   Francine, would you let the man get a word in edgewise? I want to hear who this animal friend is. Bobby who is it?

BOBBY   It's an orangutan.

GORDON   You're kidding me?

BOBBY   No, it's an orangutan.

GORDON   Of course. Why didn't I think of that? It's brilliant.

BOBBY   Okay, now we come to the love interest.

FRANCINE   That's not an orangutan too I hope.

BOBBY   No.

GORDON   And that's good, because Canadian filmgoers are cool
                to that sort of thing. I don't know what it is. Maybe
                we're not worldly, I don't know.

BOBBY   Well, no it's not an orangutan.

GORDON   Good.

BOBBY   It's an anthropologist named Jean who crash lands on
                the escarpment.

FRANCINE   Okay, that's it.

BOBBY   What?

FRANCINE   That's it.

BOBBY   Is there a problem, Francine?

FRANCINE   I'll say there's a problem. There's a big problem.

GORDON   Actually, Bobby, I'm afraid I have to side with
                Francine on this one.

FRANCINE   Well, it's about time.

GORDON   I mean, two plane crashes on the same escarpment?
                That's just too much of a coincidence for me.

BOBBY   Well, Gordon, we are talking about a twenty-year gap
                between the first one and the second one.

GORDON   A twenty-year gap?

BOBBY   Twenty years.

GORDON   Oh!

BOBBY   You didn't think they happened one after the other?

GORDON   (*laughing*) I don't know what I was thinking. So,
                there's a gap then?

FRANCINE   Gordon?

GORDON   What?

FRANCINE   Haven't you noticed?

GORDON   Noticed what?

FRANCINE   The story. It's "Tarzan".

GORDON   It's what?

FRANCINE   It's "Tarzan". The Ape Man.

GORDON   Tarzan?

FRANCINE   Yes, the escarpment. The jungle. The apes.

GORDON   Frannie, his name is Trevor. How can it be Tarzan
                when his name is Trevor?

FRANCINE   It's the same story!

BOBBY   Actually, Francine, this story has nothing to do with
                the jungle.

FRANCINE   But, you just said it was set in the jungle.

BOBBY   Yes, but you see, the jungle is merely a metaphor for
                North America's decaying inner cities, and the young
                boy represents inner city youth and the insurmountable
                odds they face as they struggle to survive in a modern
                cesspool.

GORDON   And the orangutan?

BOBBY   Is hope.

GORDON   (*to FRANCINE*) There, you see? Now, does that
                sound like "Tarzan" to you?

FRANCINE   Gordon? Tarzan and Jane? Trevor and Jean?

GORDON   Bobby, I'm sorry, but would you give us a moment
                please?

BOBBY	Hmm?
GORDON	Could you step out of the office for just a moment?
BOBBY	Oh certainly. Yes. (*he stands and moves to the office door*)
GORDON	I'm really sorry but I think Fran and I should talk.
BOBBY	No problem.
GORDON	Please forgive us.
BOBBY	I understand completely. Take all the time you need.
GORDON	Thank you. Thank you very much. (*taking the bottle from BOBBY*) Help yourself to some coffee out there if you like. It's Amaretto Almond.

BOBBY exits and closes the door.

FRANCINE	Gordon, what is wrong with you? You know bloody well that story is "Tarzan".
GORDON	I don't know anything of the sort.
FRANCINE	Oh, Gordon, come on...
GORDON	I *said* I don't know anything of the sort. Damn it, Francine, I've always wanted to be a success in this industry. I always wanted to have my name attached to a hit movie. Just one. From the first time I saw Gary Cooper in "High Noon", that's all I've wanted to do: make movies. Movies that I could be remembered for. And I'm not talking about my fifteen minutes of fame, Francine. No. I want two hours, opening nationwide on the May twenty-fourth weekend. That's what I want. And Bobby Holland is my ticket.
FRANCINE	But, Gordon, it's "Tarzan".
GORDON	No. No. I don't wanna hear that it's "Tarzan" or anything else. I don't wanna hear that. All I care about is that it's Bobby Holland. That's it.

FRANCINE   But, he's lost it, Gordon. He's fried.

GORDON   He's Bobby Holland, damn it! Bobby Holland! And I am grabbin' his coat tails and hangin' on for all I'm worth!

FRANCINE   Well, fine, but I can't go along with you on this one.

GORDON   I'd like to have you there. I mean, we're partners. Are we still partners?

FRANCINE   Not on this project, Gordon. I'm afraid I can't.

GORDON   Fine. Fine. Okay. But, you're gonna miss out, Francine. You're gonna miss out on the ride of a lifetime. (*he opens the door and calls*) Bobby? Please?

BOBBY enters the room again.

Bobby, I'm afraid Francine's decided not to join us on this particular venture.

BOBBY   Oh, I'm sorry to hear that.

GORDON   Well, she has other things that are going to be occupying her time — the Margaux Kenyon project in particular — and we don't want her attentions divided as it were.

BOBBY   Completely understandable.

FRANCINE   Before I leave though, I do have one question, Bobby. How do the apes get the name Trevor from the passport?

BOBBY   Well, that's obvious, isn't it?

FRANCINE   How?

BOBBY   Do you have a passport?

FRANCINE   Yes.

BOBBY   Does it have your name on it?

FRANCINE   Yes.

BOBBY   Well?

FRANCINE looks at GORDON.

GORDON   Makes sense to me.

FRANCINE exits.

GORDON   I'm very sorry, Bobby.

BOBBY   No problem.

GORDON   She's usually so open to new ideas.

BOBBY   People change, Gordon. It's this business.

GORDON   It's a damn shame.

BOBBY   It's sad.

GORDON   Now, please go on with the story.

BOBBY   All right. Did I mention the swinging on the vines?

GORDON   I don't think so.

BOBBY   Well, Trevor swings on these jungle vines, going from tree to tree, landing on branches. Oh, and he wrestles alligators with his bare hands. Splashing around in the water, tossing and turning, fighting for his life...

BOBBY thrashes about on the stage, acting out his ideas as GORDON looks on with some sadness. Lights down.

End.

The Agent

Time: The present.

Place: The office of literary agent, Mark Young.

As the scene opens, MARK YOUNG is talking on the phone.

MARK   Well, I know for a fact that Margaux would want to write the screenplay herself ... No, she hasn't done that sort of thing before but, hey, how difficult can it be? Stallone does it for Chrissake ...Well, of, course you're getting the rights. Why? You've heard what? .... No no, they're just a couple of hack producers. I've got a meeting with them on Monday, I'll blow them off and that'll be it.

> *He walks by his window and sees something outside. He looks out and up.*

What the hell? ... Well, there's some nut out on a ledge across the street. I don't know. He's threatening to jump I guess. Man, it tears my guts out to see someone that despondent. Who did you have in mind to direct, Michael? Who?.... (*moving away from the window*) Oh, Jesus, Bobby Holland hasn't made a picture in five years ... Well, he's a drunk ... Christ, yeah. The man's breath could fire up a barbecue.

> *ELLIE YOUNG enters the office. MARK motions for her to sit. She doesn't. Instead she begins to search through her purse.*

On the other hand, maybe it would add to the mystique of the film. (*as if he's announcing a headline*) Bobby Holland's comeback movie, you know, shit like that ... Well, hey, if the guy's got a substance-abuse problem, let's take full advantage of it. Hold on a sec, will you, Michael?' (*covering the phone*) Ellie, I'm on the phone with Disney. Just have a seat. This is very important.

> *ELLIE pulls a picture from her purse and shows it to MARK, who looks at it for a moment.*

MARK   (*into the phone*) Michael, I'm sorry. I'm going to have to call you back. Margaux's on the other line and she's got a couple more points she wants to bring to my attention ... Fifteen minutes? (*looks at his watch*) Yeah, about quarter after four. Thanks, Michael. Bye-bye. (*he hangs up*)

ELLIE   Well?

MARK   (*laughing it off*) Well, that's some photograph. Where in the heck did you get that?

ELLIE   Is that you, Mark? Is that your naked ass hanging out there?

MARK   Me? Me?! Absolutely not.

ELLIE   It's not?

MARK   No.

ELLIE   Because the man who was following you, and who took this picture, says it is you.

MARK   Well, wait a minute now. (*looks at the picture again*) Yes, that is me.

ELLIE   You bastard.

MARK   Ellie, wait a minute. Now, this can be explained quite easily.

ELLIE   Oh, can it? Well, that's good. Because I see a picture of my husband having sex in a car with another woman, and for some reason I assumed it was a bad thing. I mean, you two are having sex, aren't you? That's what it looks like. Or is this the aftermath of some freak accident where you were thrown pantsless into the back seat of her car? Thank God her naked torso was there to break your fall!

MARK   Sarcasm is not going to help here, Ellie.

ELLIE   Who is that, Mark? Is that who I think that is? Is that the wife of your best friend?

MARK   Yes.

ELLIE   And that's Henry's car, isn't it? His brand new Pontiac Grand Prix?

MARK   Yes.

ELLIE   So, you're having sex with your best friend's wife in his brand new Grand Prix. How long has this been going on, Mark?

MARK   It hasn't been going on at all. I swear. It was a one-time thing. Once.

ELLIE   Once? You do it once and it's in the parking lot at a horse track? Who picks the parking lot of a horse track for their one and only time?

MARK   Exactly! Exactly! That shows you how impromptu the whole thing was. We didn't plan it. It just happened.

ELLIE   Oh, really? And how does something like that "just happen" at a horse track? Did somebody say, "Mount up" and you misunderstood?

MARK   Ellie, there's no need to get vulgar.

ELLIE   Vulgar?! I'm staring at a picture of my husband's naked butt in the back seat of a Pontiac!

MARK	Believe me, Ellie, I didn't enjoy it. Neither one of us enjoyed it.
ELLIE	No?
MARK	No. In fact, we couldn't wait for it to finish.
ELLIE	Well, she looks like she's enjoying it. In fact, she looks like she's enjoying it more than I ever did.
MARK	So, who took the picture? Who was following me?
ELLIE	I hired a private detective.
MARK	A private detective?
ELLIE	Yes.
MARK	You hired a private detective to spy on me?
ELLIE	Yes. Dick MacFarlane.
MARK	Dick?
ELLIE	Yes.
MARK	You hired a private dick named Dick?
ELLIE	Yes.
MARK	I don't believe you.
ELLIE	I did.
MARK	What private detective is named Dick? That's like a thief named Rob.

ELLIE hands him a business card.

What's this?

ELLIE	It's his business card.

MARK   (*reading*) "Dick MacFarlane Detective Agency. If you think there's no one who can help you, you don't know Dick." You don't know Dick?

ELLIE   All right, so he's not Arthur Miller. He got the job done, didn't he?

MARK   I can't believe this. I'm shocked, Ellie. I'm genuinely shocked.

ELLIE   Shocked?!

MARK   Oh, you bet I am. Shocked and hurt. I mean, to find out that my wife would hire a private detective — a stranger — to follow me, to spy on me. It cuts me, Ellie. Cuts me to the quick. What reason could you have possibly had to mistrust me?

ELLIE   Mark, you're humping in a Pontiac.

MARK   Oh, come on, Ellie. Come on! (*pointing at the picture*) That's not sex.

ELLIE   It's not?

MARK   No.

ELLIE   That's not sex?

MARK   Of course it isn't. You know what that is?

ELLIE   (*looking at the picture*) Well, let me see. Her feet are up in the air. She's holding on for dear life. I don't know, a new midway ride?!

MARK   No, Ellie, that is one friend consoling another.

ELLIE   Consoling?

MARK   That's right. That's therapy.

ELLIE   Therapy?!   —

MARK	That's exactly what it is. I mean, she was very upset that day. Extremely upset. She told me that things with her and Henry weren't going that well. I guess Henry doesn't make love to her very often and she thinks it's because he doesn't find her attractive — so she was feeling inadequate. Well, when someone is feeling inadequate, what do you do? You try and boost their confidence. Make them feel wanted. That's what I was doing.
ELLIE	Boosting her?
MARK	Her confidence! Don't you see? She was reaching out to me. Looking for approval. I couldn't turn my back on her. I mean, if she didn't get it from me, it would've been somebody else. Anybody else. A stableboy, a jockey, the guy with one arm who sells programs. My God, in hindsight, I thank my lucky stars that I was there!
ELLIE	And where was Henry, when all of this was going on?
MARK	He was watching the race. That was the day our horse died at the three-quarter pole. That's the kind of day it was, Ellie. Emotions were at a fever pitch. That's how things like that happen. (*pointing to the picture*) Emotions get all out of whack.
ELLIE	All right, Mark, if this was a one-time thing, then how do you explain all the time you've been spending at the office lately? All the dinner meetings that keep you out late every night. How do you explain those?
MARK	How do you think I landed Margaux Kenyon as a client? Do you think things like that just happen? No. I have to wine and dine people like that. Here, you can check my week-at-a-glance. All of the appointments and dinners, they're all written down. Every one of them. Look.
ELLIE	I don't give a damn about your week-at-a-glance. You could have altered that.
MARK	Altered my week-at-a-glance?

ELLIE   Yes, altered your week-at-a-glance.

MARK   Ellie, a businessman does not alter his week-at-a-glance. It's just not done.

ELLIE   I suppose you're sleeping with her too.

MARK   Who?

ELLIE   That tramp novelist Margaux Kenyon.

MARK   No, I'm not.

ELLIE   Oh, come on. I've read her books. I can tell by the way she writes that she's a slut.

MARK   Oh, is that right?

ELLIE   That's right.

MARK   Can you also tell that she's a man?

ELLIE   You're damn right I ... what?

MARK   Margaux Kenyon is a man.

ELLIE   A man?

MARK   Yes. A guy from the suburbs who uses Margaux Kenyon as a pseudonym because he doesn't want his wife to find out that he's writing sex books.

ELLIE   You're lying.

MARK   I'm not, Ellie. I'll give you his number. You can call him up and ask him. (*beat*) Go on. I want you to.

ELLIE   I'm going home.

MARK   Ellie, no. Listen, I'll tell you what. Tonight, no late meetings, no clients, just you and me. We'll have a nice romantic dinner in front of the fire, and then we'll clear the supper dishes and have a passionate session of lovemaking right there on the table. Huh? I'll be your Mark á la carte. What do you say?

ELLIE   Well, that might be difficult, Mark.

MARK   Why?

ELLIE   The locks have been changed.

MARK   What locks?

ELLIE   The locks on the house. I had them changed after you left this morning.

MARK   What? (*laughing it off*) Well, aren't you the hotheaded one. Well, that's no problem. Don't worry about it. Just give me a spare key and I'll use that.

        ELLIE begins to go through her purse.

Boy, you really did misunderstand, didn't you? Changing the locks. Well, it's a good thing you came here today so we could get it cleared up...

        ELLIE pulls another picture out of her purse and shows it to him.

Another picture? What, is this guy working for *National Geographic*?!

ELLIE   Who's this one, Mark?

MARK   You know, Ellie, this is starting to sound a lot like nitpicking.

ELLIE   Who is it?

MARK   Who is it?

ELLIE   Who is it?

MARK   Well, once again, it can be easily explained.

ELLIE   You don't say.

MARK   Yes, you see, about a month ago, these TV people
              came sniffing around for an interview with Margaux.
              Well, of course, in order to keep my client's secret, I
              couldn't let them do that, so I turned them down. But
              this woman kept hounding me. She was relentless. It
              was terrible. So, finally I had to throw myself to this
              princess of paparazzi, in the same way a mother would
              throw herself in front of a bus to protect her child.

ELLIE   Uh-huh. So, you went swimming naked in her pool,
              after which, (*switching to another picture*) you made
              love to her in the backyard hammock.

MARK   Ellie, I'm sorry.

ELLIE   Honest to God, Mark, you are so shallow.

MARK   Shallow?

ELLIE   Yes, shallow. Your emotions are orchestrated. You use
              them as a means to an end. Nothing more.

MARK   Well, now you've really hurt me.

ELLIE   What's her name?

MARK   Why do you want to know that?

ELLIE   I'm curious.

MARK   What difference does it make?

ELLIE   You don't remember, do you?

MARK   Of course, I remember.

ELLIE   Have you slept with that many women, Mark, that
              you can't remember their names?

MARK   Of course not.

ELLIE   Well, what is it?

MARK   Let me check my week-at-a-glance.

ELLIE   It's Gerard, Mark. Like in "The Fugitive". Pam Gerard. She lives at twelve-nineteen Churchill Boulevard. I know because I just mailed copies of these photographs to her husband. Not laughing at my private dick now, are you?

She turns to leave.

MARK   Ellie, don't leave me.

ELLIE   It's too late, Mark. There's nothing you can say to make me stay now.

MARK   I'll kill myself.

ELLIE   All right, I'll stay long enough to see that, but then I have to go.

MARK   I mean it. I'll jump out of that window if you walk out of here.

ELLIE   You're on the ground floor, Mark.

MARK   All right then, I'll go up to the tenth floor and jump.

ELLIE   Let's go.

MARK   I mean it, Ellie.

ELLIE   So do I. Let's go! (*she opens the office door*)

MARK   All right. All right. You don't believe me, do you?

ELLIE   I don't believe anything you say.

MARK   Fine, I'll show you then. I'll show you. (*he moves towards the door*)

ELLIE   You'll have to take the stairs. The elevator's out.

MARK   What?

ELLIE   They were working on it as I came in.

MARK   Ten flights of stairs. I can't do that. It'll give me a heart attack.

ELLIE   What?

MARK   You know my family's history of heart disease? A climb like that would kill me.

ELLIE   Isn't that the idea?

MARK   Not from a heart attack. Those things hurt.

ELLIE   So, you're not going to jump?

MARK   Of course I am. As soon as the elevator's fixed.

ELLIE   My God, Mark. You see that? You can't even be sincere about killing yourself.

MARK   I am sincere! I mean, it Ellie! The second that elevator is working again, I'm on it! I'm riding it to the top and I'm saying good-bye!

> *ELLIE exits.*

Ellie, come back!! I can't live without you!! I won't! Ellie! (*quieter*) Ellie.

> *He waits for a second and then despondently turns back to his desk and sits. The phone rings. He answers it.*

Hello? (*suddenly perking up*) Oh, hi, Michael ... So, Bobby Holland, huh? You know the more I think about it, the more I like it. Let's give the lush a call.

> *Lights down.*

> *End.*

ACT TWO

The Visit

Time: The present.

Place: The office of lawyer RICHARD PENNY.

As the scene opens, RICHARD sits at his desk, talking on the phone.

RICHARD   Well, hopefully my meeting won't last too long. I should be at your place by five-thirty ... Mmm, I can't wait. Have the wine chilling and the Sinatra playing ... Oh, listen, I could sure use one of your fabulous back rubs tonight. Good. I've got some tension knots like you wouldn't believe ... Well, you do mine, and I'll do yours.

              The office door opens and RHONDA and LLOYD PENNY enter. RHONDA carries a picnic basket.

RHONDA   Hello, Counselor, Mind if we come in? (*they enter and close the door*)

RICHARD   (*into the phone*) I've gotta go ... Yeah, see you then. (*he hangs up the phone*) Mom, Dad, what are you doing here?

RHONDA   We brought lunch. Ooh, look at this office, Lloyd. Is this the office of a big-wheel lawyer, or what?

LLOYD   Very nice, Ricky.

RICHARD   Mom, it's three-thirty. I've already had lunch.

RHONDA	Well, so, you'll have some more. You're too thin anyway.
LLOYD	It's Lobster.
RICHARD	Lobster? You brought lobster?
RHONDA	McLobster. Your father insisted.
LLOYD	I happen to like McLobster.
RHONDA	(*to RICHARD*) I brought some vegetables and a cold plate for us, Richard.

She sets the basket on his desk.

RICHARD	Mom, really, I don't have time, I have a meeting. And how did you get by my secretary?
RHONDA	I told her I was your mother. She sent us right in. It's a woman thing. She's rather trampy looking, isn't she? (*she sits*)
RICHARD	Who, Tammy?
RHONDA	Tammy? Well, say no more. Lloyd, are you going to sit?
LLOYD	I'm looking at the office. Very nice, Ricky. And so tidy.
RHONDA	Well, Richard always was the neat one of the two boys, weren't you dear?
RICHARD	Sure. Mom, listen to me...
RHONDA	Listen nothing. You've been in this office for almost a year now and you haven't invited us to see it once. So, we're smashing.
RICHARD	Crashing.
RHONDA	Whatever. Now, sit down and have some food. Your meeting can wait twenty minutes.

RICHARD   Mom...

RHONDA   Sit.

RICHARD   All right, but just twenty minutes. That's it.

RHONDA   Right, twenty minutes. We'll wolf our food down, give ourselves heartburn, and be on our way.

LLOYD   (*not listening, he notices RICHARD's week-at-a-glance*) Nice week-at-a-glance, Ricky. Mmm, leather bound. Where'd ya get it?

RICHARD   Tammy gave it to me.

LLOYD   Nice. Oh, and what's this? (*picks up a book*) Margaux Kenyon, huh?

RHONDA   Since when did you start reading filth, Richard? Since you moved downtown?

RICHARD   I'm negotiating the movie rights for a client, Mom, that's all.

RHONDA   Oh.

RICHARD   So how are you both? What's new, Dad?

LLOYD   Saw a horse die at the track a couple of weeks ago. Terrible thing. Heart attack. Went down like he was polaxed.

RHONDA   (*unpacking the basket*) Have you got any glasses, dear? I brought orangeade.

RICHARD   Glasses? Uh, yeah. (*he gets up and gets the glasses*)

LLOYD   Don't get one for me, Ricky. That stuff gives me gas.

RHONDA   Everything gives you gas.

LLOYD   Well, this stuff especially. All that pulp.

RHONDA   What pulp? There's no pulp in orangeade.

LLOYD	There's pulp. Believe me.
RHONDA	It's made from crystals.
LLOYD	Right. Pulp crystals. So, did ya hear, Ricky? They're putting pants on the statue of Cupid.
RHONDA	Not pants, Lloyd. A loin cloth. And it's about time they put something on him. It's rude. Him standing there with his willy hanging out like that.
LLOYD	It's Cupid, Rhonda. Hanging is an overstatement. So, how's the law business, Ricky?
RICHARD	Good, Dad. It's going well.
LLOYD	Got any big cases coming up? Anything juicy? Any murders?
RICHARD	Well, I don't really get anything like that, Dad. I'm an entertainment lawyer.
RHONDA	Entertainment lawyer in Canada. There's a duck that won't float.
RICHARD	I do fine, Mom.
RHONDA	So, do you handle any big names?
RICHARD	Well, probably no big names that you'd recognize, Mom?
RHONDA	Oh, what am I, a hermit? I get out. I read the *T.V. Guide*. Now, who?
RICHARD	Uh ... well, Ralph Benmergui.
RHONDA	Who?
RICHARD	Ralph Benmergui.
RHONDA	Who's he when he's home?
LLOYD	Benmergui, he's the guy who played Ghandi?

RICHARD	No, that's Ben Kingsley.
LLOYD	Whatever.
RHONDA	All right, who else?
RICHARD	Well, a couple of film producers. Francine Majors and Gordon Blaine.
RHONDA	Never heard of them. Here, have a gherkin. (*she offers RICHARD a pickle*)
LLOYD	So, if one of your clients murdered somebody, would you defend them?
RICHARD	Probably not, no. They'd need a criminal lawyer,
LLOYD	(*disgusted*) Ahh.
RHONDA	Lloyd, eat your McLobster before it goes bad.
LLOYD	It's not gonna go bad. We just bought it.
RHONDA	Well, how do we know how fresh their food is? And when it comes to shellfish you don't wanna take chances. You could collapse from food poisoning and you'd be dead before we got you to a hospital.
LLOYD	Why do you do that to me?
RHONDA	Do what?
LLOYD	She does that to me every meal. Threatens me with my death if I don't eat everything the second it's set down in front of me,
RHONDA	Oh, nonsense. (*to RICHARD*) So, there's no change in your Aunt Sylvia's condition, in case you were going to ask, Richard.
RICHARD	Oh, I'm sorry to hear that.
RHONDA	You know they really should get her out more. I think the fresh air would do her a world of good.

RICHARD   Mom, she's in a coma.

RHONDA   We all need fresh air, Richard, coma or no coma. And
            how do we know what's going through her mind while
            she's lying there? I mean, Aunt Sylvia was very
            active. She used to go on bus tours all the time with
            her square-dancing club. I think if they loaded her on a
            bus right now it might be just the tonic she needs.
            Although to tell you the truth, I'd be thankful for
            some time off my feet like she's getting. Go go go,
            that's all I do these days. If it's not one thing, it's
            another. I'm delivering the Meals on Wheels. I'm
            volunteering at the seniors' home two hours a day.
            Oh, and now, look at this. Look what your brother
            bought for me. (*she pulls a little cellular phone out of
            her purse*) A phone of all things.

RICHARD   Neil? What'd he buy you that for?

RHONDA   He says he wants to be able to talk to me whenever he
            needs to. It's like being on call twenty-four hours a
            day. In fact, he just phoned me as we were coming
            over.

LLOYD   Five times he's called her today.

RICHARD   Well, he's going through a tough time, Dad.

LLOYD   Ahhh. (*he sits*)

RHONDA   Well, I say he should get over it. We all have. And
            this therapy business. I don't know about that.

LLOYD   They're crooks, these therapists.

RICHARD   I think he needs it, Mom. I really do.

RHONDA   You know what he said to me yesterday? Here, have
            some Polish coil. (*she holds up a coil of Polish
            sausage*)

RICHARD   No, thanks.

RHONDA	So, anyway, he said to me, Neil did, he said I was overbearing. Domineering. Do you believe that?
RICHARD	Well...
RHONDA	I'm not the one calling him five times a day. He's calling me. And once would be plenty enough, believe me. Domineering.
RICHARD	Well, Mom...
RHONDA	Use a serviette, dear, your gherkin's dripping. Honestly, you're worse than the seniors.
RICHARD	Mom, if you want the truth, you are a little overbearing.

> *There is a pause as RICHARD and LLOYD fear the worst.*

RHONDA	What?
LLOYD	(*changing the subject*) What's the rent like for an office like this, Ricky?
RHONDA	Lloyd, do you, mind? We're having a discussion here?
LLOYD	Sorry.
RHONDA	(*to RICHARD*) What do you mean, overbearing? I let you kids choose your own careers. I didn't interfere in any way, did I, Lloyd?
LLOYD	She's right, Ricky. We stayed the hell out of your lives as best we could.
RHONDA	Well, I wouldn't go that far. We took an interest.
LLOYD	Just saying what I thought you wanted to hear, dear.
RHONDA	Domineering. That's ridiculous. I mean, you're not gay, are you?
RICHARD	What?

RHONDA	Gay.
RICHARD	I don't understand.
RHONDA	Well, if I was a domineering mother, chances are, you'd be gay.
RICHARD	What? That has nothing to do with being gay.
RHONDA	Oh no? What about that Hilyard boy down the street from us? What's his name,
LLOYD	Ty.
RHONDA	Ty Hilyard. His mother does that gardening show on T.V.
LLOYD	"Digging With Daphne".
RHONDA	That's the one. Well, he's gay. And she's very domineering.
LLOYD	She's a ball-buster.
RHONDA	Liberace was another one. Don't ask me why, but for some reason if you look behind a gay man, you'll find an overbearing mother.
LLOYD	That isn't all you'll find.
RHONDA	Lloyd, please.
RICHARD	Mom, that is just not so. I'm sorry.
RHONDA	Well, you can believe it or not, but the fact remains that if I was a domineering mother, you'd stand a very good chance of being gay. And if you're gay, I'm Arnold Schwarzennegger.
RICHARD	Well, Arnie, I'm afraid I've got some news for you.
RHONDA	(*beat*) What?
RICHARD	Well...

RHONDA Well what? What?

RICHARD I guess this is as good a time as any to tell you two. I mean, you brought it up,

RHONDA What are you saying? Lloyd, what's he saying?

LLOYD He's kidding. He's having fun with you. (*he picks up his McLobster*)

RICHARD No, Dad, It's true. I'm ... uh ... I'm gay.

> *Pause, as LLOYD is about to take a bite, the moment is frozen. RHONDA takes out her phone and dials.*

Mom, what are you doing?

RHONDA I'm calling the hospital. I'm going to tell them to have a respirator ready because I'll be there in ten minutes.

RICHARD Mom, stop. (*he takes the phone from her*)

RHONDA Oh, this is a fine welcome to your new office, isn't it? Thank-you very much.

RICHARD Well, I had to tell you sometime.

LLOYD No, you didn't.

RHONDA When did this happen?

RICHARD It doesn't happen, Mom. It just ... it's there.

LLOYD I can't eat now. (*puts his food down*)

RICHARD Dad...

LLOYD Three ninety-nine I paid for that and I can't eat it.

RICHARD Dad, don't be like that. It doesn't change anything. I'm still the same son you've always had.

LLOYD	You're a lawyer, for Godssake! You know what happens to gay lawyers. You saw "Philadelphia". Jesus!
RHONDA	Lloyd, don't curse in here. It's a law office. So, Richard. You're gay.
RICHARD	Yes.
RHONDA	Hm-hm. So, you know what that means, don't you?
RICHARD	What?
RHONDA	I'm domineering.
RICHARD	No, it doesn't mean that.
RHONDA	Oh, yes it does. So, Neil was right.
LLOYD	Does Neil know?
RICHARD	Yes, he's known for quite some time.
RHONDA	Well, that explains a lot.
RICHARD	About what?
RHONDA	About his mental condition. Holding this secret in all this time. Betraying his mother and father.
RICHARD	He wasn't betraying you. I asked him not to say anything until I told you.
RHONDA	So, I suppose he's gay too, is he?
RICHARD	No, he's not.
LLOYD	What do you mean he's not?
RICHARD	He's not.
LLOYD	You mean, you're gay and your brother, the figure skater, is straight?! What the hell kind of world is this?

RICHARD	Dad, you're stereotyping.
LLOYD	Well, excuse me for being from another generation.
RICHARD	I'm afraid that is no excuse.
RHONDA	Don't talk to your father that way. And drink your orangeade.
RICHARD	Mom, I have to go. Really.
LLOYD	What, you drop this bombshell on us and now you're gonna leave?
RICHARD	I have a meeting. We'll talk later.
LLOYD	No, we'll talk now.
RHONDA	Oh, let him go, Lloyd. This is nothing that can't wait. Two days from now, three days, he'll still be gay. (*to RICHARD*) Will you?
RICHARD	Yes, Mom, I will. (*he picks up his brief case*) Now, I'll call you tomorrow and I'll come over for dinner. (*he kisses RHONDA*) You can see yourselves out?
RHONDA	Yes.
RICHARD	Fine.
RHONDA	You want to take something with you? A radish?
RICHARD	No, I'm fine. See you later, Dad. (*he moves to the door*)
RHONDA	Richard?

RICHARD stops.

Are you seeing anyone? (*beat*) I'd like to know.

RICHARD	Yes, I am.
RHONDA	Is he a nice man?

RICHARD	Yes, he's very nice.
RHONDA	Well, you can bring him to dinner if you like.
LLOYD	(*almost to himself*) Wooo!
RICHARD	(*beat*) Is that all right with you, Dad?

LLOYD doesn't answer.

RHONDA	Lloyd?
LLOYD	Ahh, all right, but ... behave yourselves.
RICHARD	What's that supposed to mean?
LLOYD	I don't know what it means. Parents use it for everything. Fine, bring your friend over.
RICHARD	Thanks, Dad. I'll see you later. Good-bye, Mom.

RICHARD exits.

LLOYD	Well, you're taking this calmly.
RHONDA	(*packing the picnic basket*) Oh, you know Richard. He's gone through phases all his life. This is just another one.
LLOYD	Rhonda, I may be a little ignorant in this area, but I don't think this kind of thing is a phase.
RHONDA	No, you'll see. He'll try it for a while and then he'll move on to something else. Ham radios. Scuba diving.
LLOYD	Rhonda, come on.
RHONDA	Can we just not talk about it please?
LLOYD	You *are* upset.
RHONDA	Of course I'm upset. To find out at this stage in my life that I'm domineering? Wouldn't you be upset?

LLOYD   Maybe I should've played catch with the boy more often.

RHONDA   Oh, you've got nothing to do with this. It's all maternal. Don't ask me to explain it. I mean, a mother takes her little boy and cares for him, picks him up and dusts him off when he falls, kisses his hurt when he gets a scrape, shows him how to bake a bundt cake so it comes out moist and fluffy, and what happens? I didn't know I was being overbearing. I was only doing what my mother did for me, and her mother for her and hers for her.

LLOYD   What is this, "Roots"?

RHONDA   Never mind. Just take me home please. I'd like to lie down. And there's another thing. What am I supposed to serve him and his friend? What do these people eat?

LLOYD   They're not tropical fish, Rhonda. They eat what we eat.

RHONDA   Overbearing. Domineering. Who would've guessed? (*she exits*)

                              LLOYD picks up the Margaux Kenyon book and looks at the cover.

RHONDA   (*off*) Lloyd!!

LLOYD   Coming.

                              He exits. Lights down.

                              End.

The Dismissal

Time: The present.

Place: The office of racetrack manager STAN THURBER.

STAN   Five thirty. Good. And we'll spend a nice quiet evening alone ... You know I will. Back rub? No problem. The doctor is in. You've got tension knots? I've got knots that could earn me a Boy Scout badge Do mine and I'll do yours. I was just going to say that. All right. See you in a couple of hours.

STAN hangs up and looks out the window. There is a knock at the door. Without looking around he answers.

Yes?

The door opens and ARTIE BARNES enters. He's wearing jeans, a jean jacket over a shirt, and a cowboy hat.

ARTIE   You wanted to see me, Stan?

STAN   (*turning to look at ARTIE*) Oh, Artie, yes. Come on in.

ARTIE enters and closes the door.

ARTIE   Doing a little daydreaming?

STAN   Hmm? Oh, yes. Well, sometimes I like to look out there and just watch the place operate, you know?

ARTIE   Yeah, I don't blame you. You must be pretty proud.

STAN   Well, we're not the biggest outfit on the circuit but, by God, we try the hardest.

ARTIE   It's a great place to be. There's no doubt about that. Great place to work. You feel like you're part of a family here.

STAN   Sit down, Artie, please.

ARTIE   Thanks. (*ARTIE sits*) Man, this is some desk. Absolutely beautiful. Your father had good taste in furnishings, I'll say that.

STAN   Oh, that he did.

ARTIE   And you keep it nice and tidy too. Good. Yeah, I remember when my Dad used to bring me in here when I was a kid, and your father would sit there in that chair, and they'd talk and laugh across this desk.

STAN   Yeah, they were good friends all right. (*he sits in his chair*)

ARTIE   They were best friends. Went through the war together, got married in a double ceremony together. Hell, they were inseparable. I mean, it was across this desk that your Dad promised my Dad that he'd find a place for me here one day. And he did too. Just before he died. Hired me right on, doing what I'd always dreamed of doing. He was a man of his word, Stan. He was a dying breed. (*correcting himself*) Well, I don't mean he was a dying breed because he was dying. I don't mean that. I mean, sure, he was dying, but that's not what I'm saying...

STAN   I know what you're saying, Artie. He was one of a kind.

ARTIE   That's exactly what he was.

STAN   Well, no one knows that better than I, believe me. But, he's been gone for two years now and, well, life goes on, you know?

ARTIE	Absolutely.
STAN	And it's time for me to move on too. To take this operation that my Dad built from his own sweat, and forge ahead with it. Improve on it even.
ARTIE	Well, I don't know how you could improve on it, Stan. I honestly don't.
STAN	Uh-huh. Artie, I've asked you to come in today because there's something I want to talk to you about.
ARTIE	Sure, Stan. What is it?
STAN	Well, Artie, to tell you the truth, I've been getting some complaints
ARTIE	Complaints?
STAN	Yeah.
ARTIE	What complaints? Not about me?
STAN	I'm afraid so.
ARTIE	You've gotta be kiddin' me. What kind of complaints? From who?
STAN	From the owners mainly.
ARTIE	The owners? What could the owners have to complain about?
STAN	Oh, I think you can guess, Artie.
ARTIE	No. I have no idea. I mean, I give them a hundred percent every time out. I give them my all, you know that.
STAN	No, they're not complaining about the effort. We all know you're trying, Artie,
ARTIE	Well, what is it then?

STAN   Artie, come on.

ARTIE   What?!

STAN   Artie?

ARTIE   No, what?

STAN   I think we've avoided the issue long enough.

ARTIE   What issue?

STAN   Artie, how much do you weigh?

ARTIE   A hundred and twelve pounds.

STAN   I beg your pardon?

ARTIE   A hundred and twelve.

STAN   Artie, you don't weigh a hundred and twelve pounds.

ARTIE   I weigh a hundred and twelve.

STAN   You're two hundred, if you're an ounce.

ARTIE   All right, a hundred and fifteen maybe. One twenty
              soaking wet.

STAN   Artie, who are we kidding?

ARTIE   What?

STAN   Come on! We tried to make it work. We did. But, it's
              time to face the facts.

ARTIE   Facts about what? What the hell are you talking
              about?

STAN   Artie, you're too big.

ARTIE   I'm what?

STAN   You're too big.

ARTIE	I'm big?
STAN	You're big.
ARTIE	I'm not big. I'm average.
STAN	Artie, you're big.
ARTIE	The hell, I'm big. There are thousands of guys out there my size. Hundreds of thousands. Millions!
STAN	Yeah, but they're not jockeys. You, you're a jockey.
ARTIE	Is this what the owners are complaining about?
STAN	Profusely.
ARTIE	But, Stan, look...
STAN	No, Artie, you look. Like I said, we're a small track here, but we're the only one of it's kind in North America. The only track that supplies the jockeys. I mean, at all the other tracks the owners have to find their own jockeys, right? Well, here they don't. That's our drawing power. And, quite frankly, Artie, the owners that are getting you assigned to their mounts ... well, they're not entirely satisfied.
ARTIE	They're sore losers, Stan. That's all it is. Their horse loses a race and they need someone to blame it on.
STAN	Artie, you haven't won a race in two years.
ARTIE	So, I've had some tough rides.
STAN	You haven't finished in the money in two years.
ARTIE	Well, you know why? Because I've been getting nags, that's why.
STAN	Artie, you've had some fine horses under you. Some very good horses.
ARTIE	Name one.

STAN	Jacob's Ladder. A quality animal.
ARTIE	He ran a bad race. He didn't save anything for the stretch.
STAN	He didn't have anything left for the stretch! He was exhausted from carrying you around, for Godssake. And what about Royal Dutchman?
ARTIE	He was a quitter.
STAN	He died! His heart gave out at the three quarter pole! You were too much weight for him.
ARTIE	That horse had congenital heart disease, Stan, and you know it. The doctor said he had a cholesterol buildup the size of Mount Pinatubo.
STAN	Cholesterol from what? He ate hay all day!
ARTIE	Well, I threw him a nice wake, didn't I?
STAN	You killed him!!
ARTIE	I resent this, Stan. I resent you implying that I'm too big.
STAN	Artie, I'm not implying. I'm telling you outright. I mean, the other jockeys weigh a hundred and nine, hundred and ten.
ARTIE	I'm big boned.
STAN	You're big! You're just big! You're too big! I mean, look at the riding outfits. They look ridiculous on you. The sleeves are up to here. (*indicates halfway up to his elbow*) The helmet sits up there like a little beanie. Artie, enough is enough, I can't stand by and let you embarrass yourself anymore.
ARTIE	Embarrass myself?
STAN	Yes.
ARTIE	I'm an embarrassment?

STAN	Artie...
ARTIE	Is that what I am?
STAN	Artie, it's not working out. That's all I meant.
ARTIE	Are you saying you don't want me to ride here anymore? Are you saying that your father's promise to my father means nothing all of a sudden?
STAN	I just think you should consider another line of work.
ARTIE	Another line of work? Like what? What's a person like me supposed to do, Stan? What?
STAN	I don't know. Professional wrestling maybe. I'm not in the job placement business, Artie. I'm in the horse racing business, and I'm telling you that it's been my experience that not many jockeys your size become successful.
ARTIE	Not many?
STAN	Very few?
ARTIE	But, some.
STAN	None. In fact, there are no jockeys your size, Artie. You're it. The "big jockey" bell curve is graded on you and you alone.
ARTIE	Uh-huh. I see.
STAN	I'm sorry.
ARTIE	(*beat*) Well, maybe I should call a lawyer.
STAN	What for?
ARTIE	Legal action. I could file a size discrimination suit against you and your track, Stan. And believe me, I'd have a case.
STAN	Well, that's your choice, Artie.

ARTIE	You're damn right it is! You're damn right. But, I won't, Stan. No, in your father's memory, I won't.
STAN	Well, I appreciate that, Artie. I really do.
ARTIE	Your father was a gentleman. He knew how to treat people. I'll tell you something, Stan. If you were half the man your father was, you wouldn't do this.
STAN	And if you were half the man *your* father was, you'd be the right size!
ARTIE	Oh, I see. This is all a big joke to you, isn't it?
STAN	No...
ARTIE	Oh, sure! You sit here in your fancy office with your big desk, and your big chair and your leather-bound week-at-a-glance. You're enjoying this.
STAN	Artie, that's not true.
ARTIE	What do you expect me to do? Do you expect me to beg?
STAN	No.
ARTIE	Because I won't. I don't beg any man for anything.
STAN	Artie, I don't want you to beg. Now, please, why don't you just go and clean out your locker?
ARTIE	Just like that, huh? Just clean out the locker and throw all of my memories into a tattered old gym bag.
STAN	Memories of what, Artie? Of staring at a pack of horses' behinds every afternoon?
ARTIE	Boy, you don't pull any punches, do you?

STAN   Artie, what do you want me to say? Do you want me to say, "Hang around for a few weeks until you find something else?" I don't think you want me to say that. That would be extremely uncomfortable for both of us. Extremely uncomfortable.

ARTIE   Who are you gonna get to take my place?

STAN   Now, why do you want to know that?

ARTIE   I'm curious.

STAN   What does it matter who we get?

ARTIE   I think I deserve to know.

STAN   Artie...

ARTIE   Come on, who?!

STAN   Well, I was thinking of Linda Sanchez.

ARTIE   Linda Sanchez?

STAN   Yeah.

ARTIE   (*acting as if he's caught on to something*) Ooooh. Oh, I see. Oh, yeah, I get it now, I'm not a victim of my size at all, am I? No, I'm a victim of sex discrimination. Of male down-sizing. Oh, I should've known.

STAN   Artie, don't be silly.

ARTIE   Man, I can't believe this. I ... you know what my dream is, Stan? Huh? My dream is to ride in the Derby one day. That's right. That's all I've ever dreamed about. Ever. The Kentucky Derby.

STAN   Artie, it's three-thirty. I'm really backed up here.

ARTIE   You think it's ridiculous, don't you? Me riding in the Derby.

STAN	Yes, I do.
ARTIE	You do?
STAN	Yes.
ARTIE	No seriously. Be honest, Stan. You can't see me in the Kentucky Derby?
STAN	No. The Kentucky Fried Chicken maybe.
ARTIE	My God, you're cold-hearted.
STAN	You asked me.
ARTIE	So, you could've lied! You could've thrown me a bone!
STAN	Artie, we all have dreams, but for some of us they just don't come true. Me, I wanted to be the next Sinatra. But, I'm not, am I? No. Some of us just don't make the dream come true, but we get over it. We move on.
ARTIE	(*beat*) Did I tell you? I'm going into therapy?
STAN	What?
ARTIE	That's right. I start today. I've got an appointment at four o'clock.
STAN	What for?
ARTIE	Well, with this losing streak I'm on, I'm starting to feel inadequate.
STAN	Well, there, you see, Artie? You see?
ARTIE	But, if I can keep at it, Stan, if I can get that one victory under my belt, I think I can turn it around.
STAN	Artie, no.
ARTIE	You'd be helping me out, Stan. You'd be getting me over the hump.

STAN	Artie, you *are* the hump.
ARTIE	Damn it, Stan, you can't do this. We go way back. We were kids together. We were best friends.
STAN	No, we weren't. That was our fathers.
ARTIE	And us too.
STAN	No, Artie. We were never best friends.
ARTIE	We weren't?
STAN	No.
ARTIE	But I liked you.
STAN	Well, that's nice.
ARTIE	You didn't like me?
STAN	Artie, I was your babysitter, My father made me play with you because there was no one else there for you. That's it.
ARTIE	You mean, you hung out with me because you had to.
STAN	I was paid to.
ARTIE	I thought we were best friends.
STAN	Well, I'm afraid not.
ARTIE	But ... but, how could I think that? How could I think one thing when the opposite was true? Oh, my God. Do you know what this does? This changes my whole childhood. Not only is a dream being shattered here but I'm losing childhood memories too. They're all tainted now.
STAN	Look, I've really got a mess of work to get to here...
ARTIE	All right. All right. You want me to beg? All right, I'm begging.

STAN	Artie, I don't want you to beg. Please.
ARTIE	No, I'm begging. Here, you've taken away my childhood, you've taken away my dreams, you might as well take my dignity too. Here you go. (*he falls to his knees*) There. A man is begging you. Is that what you want?
STAN	Artie, will you stop this?!
ARTIE	(*he leans forward and pounds the desk*) Damn it, Stan, your father hired me, himself! Right here. Do you understand. I'm talking about your father. There were promises made across this desk!
STAN	I know that, Artie, I know! But, I can't spend the rest of my life honouring my father's promises. I've got a racetrack to run, and I've got to do it the best way I know how. My way. Now, that's all I have to say on the matter. That's it.
ARTIE	Okay. Okay, fine. Fine. (*He stands*) I'll get my stuff and I'll go.
STAN	I think that would be best. And good luck with the therapy, Artie. I hope it helps.
	STAN hold his hand out to ARTIE. ARTIE doesn't shake it.
ARTIE	Yeah. God, I haven't felt this empty since what happened to my dog, Lucky, when I was eight years old.
STAN	Yeah, that was terrible, him running onto the track and getting trampled that way.
ARTIE	Trampled? Dad told me he ran away.
STAN	Yeah, well, he didn't get very far.
ARTIE	Oh, mother of God!

> *ARTIE exits. STAN looks at his watch. he*
> *moves to the coat rack, takes the trenchcoat*
> *off of the rack and throws it over his shoulder*
> *and, á la Sinatra, he sings as he exits.*

STAN   "That's life. That's what all the people say. You're
ridin' high in April, shot down in May."

> *Lights down.*

The Analyst

Time: The present.

Place: The office of analyst Sharon Freeman.

As the scene opens SHARON FREEMAN is lying on her couch.

SHARON Neil? ... Neil, come inside, would you please? I mean, I've worked very hard to build up a good reputation in the psychiatric community, Neil, and it's not exactly a feather in my cap to have a nut on my ledge? Not that you are a nut, I'm not saying you're a nut. You're just experiencing an intellective setback. (*checks her watch*) Neil, please, my four o'clock is going to be here any minute. Your time is up. If you stay out there any longer, I'm going to have to charge you for the whole hour ... All right, Neil, listen. I'm going to share something personal with you. If I share something personal with you, will you come in? You see, I'm unattached, Neil. Extremely unattached. What I'm trying to say is, I ... I haven't been ... with a man for over a year. That's right, twelve months, Neil. And that causes anxiety. Frustration. I mean, I'm as frustrated as an Avon Lady in Mennonite country. And very tense. I'm very tense these days. Yesterday I picked a fight with a Goodwill canvasser. But that's about to change, Neil. Oh, yes. You see, a couple of weeks ago I met a man. A nice man. A man I really like. And he likes me. And this afternoon at five o'clock, we're going away to a secluded lake, and do you know what we're going to do all weekend, Neil? Well, let's put it this way. If the cabin's rockin', don't bother knockin'. So, what do you say, Neil? How 'bout you just get the hell inside, huh?

NEIL   (*off*) Would you be quiet in there?! I'm on the phone
              with my mother!

SHARON   You're what? (*she looks out the window*) You've got a
              phone out there?! Oh, for Godssake, Well, that does it.
              That does it! Now hear this, Neil. I am leaving at five
              o'clock sharp, and if you're not off that ledge by then,
              one way or the other, then you are locked in for the
              weekend, buster!

                         *A man enters the office. He carries a briefcase
                         with him. He wears a suit.*

MAN   Dr. Freeman?

SHARON   What??!! Oh, I'm sorry. You must be Mr. Barnes.

MAN   I'm sorry?

SHARON   Well, uh ... come in, please. I'm sort of in the middle
              of something here. But it's nothing we can't work
              around.

MAN   Oh ... uh, all right.

SHARON   I'm Sharon Freeman.

MAN   How do you do?

                         He shakes her hand.

SHARON   Well, time will tell.

MAN   Isn't that the truth.

SHARON   Sit, please.

MAN   Thank you.

SHARON   Arthur Barnes, yes. Let me get a clean file out for you.
              (*she gets a file folder from a drawer*) Now, when we
              spoke on the phone, you said you'd never been in
              analysis before, is that right?

MAN	I beg your pardon?
SHARON	On the phone, you said this was your first time.
MAN	Is that what I said? Well, yes it is, yes. That's correct. Uh, I've never believed in the process actually.
SHARON	I see.
MAN	Always thought it was a lot of bunk, if you'll pardon my French.
SHARON	Uh-huh, and what changed your mind?
MAN	Well ... uh ... What changed my mind?
SHARON	Yes.
MAN	Well, uh ... I've come across a problem, Doctor. A problem that I can't seem to rectify by myself.
SHARON	I see. All right then, that's probably a good place to start. What is the problem?
MAN	Well... (*noticing a book on SHARON's desk, he picks it up*) Oh, Margaux Kenyon, huh? Oooh. Yeah, my wife reads her material all the time. All the time. An acquaintance of mine is her agent.
SHARON	Really?
MAN	Yeah. (*reads the title*) "My Summer In Venice". What would that be about?
SHARON	Well, actually, Venice is just a metaphor for the heroine's escape from her dreary marriage. She takes long baths and imagines it's a gondola ride along the canals of Venice.
MAN	What's so special about a gondola ride?

SHARON   Well, she ... she's with her lover, you see — Alberto.
                A young, strapping, olive-skinned Italian man. (*she
                starts to imagine it*) and Alberto makes uninhibited,
                passionate love to her, right there on the floor of the
                gondola, as it floats gingerly down the canal, their
                sensual secret betrayed only by a gentle pitching to and
                fro of the vessel.

MAN   I hear there's raw sewage in those canals.Terrible thing.

SHARON   (*snapping out of it*) Yes. Now, you were going to tell
                me about your problem.

MAN   Uh ... yeah, well, I'm feeling a certain amount of
                stress lately because of ... well, quite candidly, Doctor,
                it's my wife. You see, the quandary is that Tammy —
                that's my wife — Tammy is somewhat younger than
                I.

SHARON   How much younger?

MAN   She's twenty-eight. So you know, it's the old story.
                Older man, younger woman. She approaching her
                sexual peak, me looking at mine in the rearview
                mirror. It's extremely difficult. There's a lot of pressure
                on me.

SHARON   Pressure in what way?

MAN   In what way? Well, when it comes time to, you know,
                plant the turnip.

SHARON   I see.

MAN   When I need to park the station-wagon, if you know
                what I'm saying.

SHARON   Yes.

MAN   When it's time to raise the flag and see who salutes it.

SHARON   I understand, Mr. Barnes.

MAN   I mean, I can't compete anymore. If sex was the Olympics, I'd be Paraguay.

SHARON   So, sex is the main area of concern?

MAN   Well, yes. I mean, it's like a horse race, you know? I'm the older horse, she's the two-year-old. She's still going strong at the finish line, and it's all I can do to get into the starting gate.

SHARON   A horse race. Very insightful.

MAN   Oh, hey don't get me started on horses. No ma'am. I mean, that's another reason I'm stressed out.

SHARON   Why's that?

MAN   Well, a few months ago, this friend of mine, the agent, he inquires as to whether I might go halves with him on a racehorse. So, stupid me I say yeah, and I give him ten thousand dollars and we purchase the horse. So two weeks ago I go to the track to see my horse run, and, as they're coming on to the track before the race, I look down at my equine investment and I see this ... this giant jockey. Guy must've weighed three hundred pounds, and I'll be damned if he isn't on my horse. So, I start yelling at the guy, I'm saying "Hey, Gulliver! Get the hell off my horse!" But, he can't hear me, and I'm looking around for my partner but he's suddenly absent. So, the race starts, the horse gets three quarters of the way around the track and bing! Heart gives out. He goes down like a two-dollar hooker. And me? I'm in arrears to the tune of ten thousand dollars. Oh, and to top it off, while I'm at the track, some smart-ass kids break into my brand new Pontiac Grand Prix and leave footprints all over the inside of the roof and on the dash. What kind of monsters would do something like that?

SHARON   It's a strange world, Mr. Barnes.

MAN   You can say that again.

SHARON   So, getting back to your problem, are you saying that
            you're having trouble performing?

MAN   Well, not exactly. I can still perform. I'm just not
            doing two shows nightly anymore.

SHARON   I see. And are you worried that your wife will seek
            satisfaction elsewhere? Say, an office romance? Does
            your wife work?

MAN   Yeah, she works for this lawyer. But, he's as gay as a
            Christmas carol.

SHARON   I see.

MAN   Oh, yeah, there's no worry there.

SHARON   Good. And what do you do for a living?

MAN   I'm in sales.

SHARON   Oh. What do you sell?

MAN   Oh, listen, in my life I've sold just about everything.
            Kitchen appliances, furniture. I even sold erotic
            undergarments for a while. That's how I came to meet
            Tammy.

SHARON   And what are you selling now?

MAN   You really want to know?

SHARON   Sure.

                  The man reaches into his briefcase.

MAN   Well, Sharon — can I call you Sharon?

SHARON   If you like.

MAN   Well, Sharon, it's an all-purpose, deluxe edition,
            leather-bound, week-at-a-glance.

                  He pulls out a week-at-a-glance.

SHARON   Very nice.

MAN   Oh, very nice doesn't do it justice, Sharon. Just take a look at that. (*he hands her the week-at-a-glance*) Not only does it serve as a daily reminder three hundred and sixty-five days of the year, but it's also got a calculator built right into the inside cover. Looky there.

SHARON   Well...

MAN   You know, we were talking about reading earlier, Sharon, and for people like you and me who are constantly on the go, this is the perfect companion for those down times. That ten or fifteen minutes you get to yourself in the run of a busy day, (*turning a page in the book*) Look at this. What do you see there?

SHARON   Uh ... it looks like ... *The Bible*.

MAN   Not the entire *Bible*, Sharon, but more than enough to give you comfort and solace during those short breaks. That's right. Genesis through Ezekial, inclusive. Now, the reason they've only gone up to Ezekial is twofold. First of all, by cutting the volume down, they've saved the consumer money on the purchase price. Secondly, Sharon, quite frankly, after Ezekial, the thing starts to repeat itself.

SHARON   Are you trying to sell me a week-at-a-glance, Mr. Barnes?

MAN   Do you have one? I don't see one.

SHARON   I have an appointment book.

MAN   And that would've been more than enough ten years ago, but today's professional needs a more complete scheduling device. Look at this. (*showing her the week-at-a-glance*) it has a place for addresses, phone numbers, fax numbers, and all of the city's self-help and support groups are listed alphabetically from Alcoholics Anonymous to Zen Buddhists Without Partners. It is all you'll ever need, but it's not all you get. (*goes to his briefcase*) No, Sharon, listen to this.

If you're interested in buying today, I am authorized to include, at no additional cost, this commemorative John Diefenbaker pen and pencil set. Now, the cost of the week-at-a-glance, complete with the calculator. *The Bible*, and the pen and pencil set, is only forty-seven ninety-five. What do you think of that? Wait a minute, wait a minute, wait a minute! What did I say? Did I say forty-seven ninety-five? What am I talking about? I've come in here, I've taken up your valuable time. Never mind the forty-seven ninety-five, Sharon. The company can shoot me down like a dog if they want to, but I'll let you have it for thirty-five dollars. Thirty-five dollars, Sharon, to keep your life in order and your spiritual feet on solid ground!!

SHARON   You didn't come in here for help at all, did you?

MAN   I beg your pardon?

SHARON   The story about your wife, and your stress? That was all fabricated, wasn't it? That was just to get you in the door.

MAN   No, not at all. That story is true. Every word of it. But, I thought, as long as I'm here, why not kill two birds with one stone?

SHARON   I'm going to have to ask you to leave, Mr. Barnes.

MAN   But, I'm not finished.

SHARON   No, I'm afraid you are.

MAN   No, please, Sharon just give me a few more minutes.

SHARON   Good day, Mr. Barnes.

NEIL   (*off*) Hello???

MAN   What was that?

SHARON   Nothing.

NEIL   (*off*) Hello in there!! I'm off the phone and I'm thinking of jumping now!

SHARON   That's wonderful, Neil.

MAN   Oh, my God. Is there someone on the ledge?

SHARON   Yes, but it's nothing to worry about.

MAN   Nothing to worry about? Who is it, a patient of yours?

SHARON   Yes.

MAN   Well, I'll be damned. What's his problem?

SHARON   He's a figure skater. The one who fell during the Olympics.

MAN   He fell? And he needs therapy for that?

SHARON   Well, he fell seven times. Once stepping onto the ice, four times during the program, once again as he was leaving the ice, and then one final time as he was being interviewed on network television. Now, have a nice day, Mr. Barnes.

NEIL   (*off*) I mean it! I'm jumping!

SHARON   Oh, for Godssake, shut up! Honestly. Me, me, me. Other people have lives too, you know! And some of us would like to get on with them!!

NEIL   (*off*) You're not very nice,

SHARON   You want nice? I'll show you nice! Come over here you little Ice Capades reject! Come here!

She reaches out the window.

MAN   Is this some new kind belligerence therapy?

SHARON   (*moving away from the window*) No, no. It's just that I finally clear my schedule so that I can have a weekend to myself to look after my own mental

	health, and what happens? God, I am so sick of these dime-a-dozen neurotics.
NEIL	(*off*) I am not a dime a dozen!!
SHARON	Shut up!!
MAN	And you can't talk him in?
SHARON	No, I've been trying for a half an hour now and nothing.
MAN	Let me try.
SHARON	What?
MAN	Let me give it a try.
SHARON	Mr. Barnes, you're not qualified. You're not a psychiatrist.
MAN	No, but I'm one helluva salesman. (*beat, as SHARON thinks about it*) What could it hurt?
SHARON	(*beat*) Okay. Go ahead.
MAN	And if I can talk him in, will you buy the week-at-a-glance?
SHARON	Listen, if you can talk him in before five o'clock, I'll buy one for everybody on this floor.
MAN	Lady, you're on! (*the man moves to the window*) Hey, Neil? Hi. How ya doin' buddy?
NEIL	(*off*) Who the hell are you?
MAN	I'm a friend, Neil. A friend of the common man. Listen, do you mind if I come out there with you? I'm a big believer in level playing fields.
NEIL	(*off*) Do whatever you like.

MAN	There you go. (*he climbs out and moves to the opposite side of the window that NEIL is on*) Hey, look. Television cameras. Wave, Neil. (*yelling to the cameras*) Hello!! It's okay!! We're fine!!
	RHONDA and LLOYD PENNY enter the office.
RHONDA	Neil? (*to SHARON*) Where's my son?
SHARON	He's on the ledge. Please, Mrs. Penny, don't upset him.
LLOYD	Upset him? He's on the ledge, isn't he?!
	RHONDA rushes to the window.
RHONDA	Neil? Neil, it's mother. (*she looks to the side where the MAN is standing*) I'm here, darling.
MAN	(*off*) Good afternoon.
RHONDA	Who are you? (*to SHARON*) That's not my son. Who the hell is that?
MAN	(*off*) Arthur Barnes.
RHONDA	What?
MAN	(*off*) The name's Arthur Barnes. (*the MAN's hand reaches down to shake RHONDA's*) Pleased to meet you.
RHONDA	(*bewildered*) Likewise.
NEIL	(*off*) Mother?
RHONDA	Neil? (*she looks out the window*) Neil, what are you doing out here with a stranger?
NEIL	(*off*) Mother, I'm not having a good day.

RHONDA   You're not having a good day? Your brother, the
                lawyer, just told me he's gay. What kind of day do you
                think I'm having? Maybe you can tell me, Neil. Why
                does a man wait until he's in his thirties to tell his
                parents that he's gay?

NEIL   (*off*) Because he's scared of you, Mother. We all are.

LLOYD   Hey? That'll be enough of that, young man! Your
                mother's done her best raising you! We both have! And
                what did it get us? Public humiliation on national
                television!

RHONDA   Good, Lloyd, Why don't you just reach out there and
                give him a shove?

LLOYD   Ahhh!

MAN   (*off*) What's his name?

RHONDA   What?

MAN   (*off*) Your gay son. The lawyer. What's his name?

RHONDA   Richard, Richard Penny.

MAN   (*off*) Get out of here! Well, talk about your small
                world. My wife works for him.

RHONDA   Your wife?

MAN   (*off*) Her name is Tammy. She's his secretary,

RHONDA   Oh, Tammy. Yes, I met her. Nice looking girl. (*she
                throws SHARON a look*) If you like that look. (*to
                MAN*) Now, you, Mister whatever-your-name-is, can I
                talk to my son alone, please?

MAN   (*appearing in the window*) Actually, Mrs. Penny, I
                wonder if you could give Neil and me a couple of
                minutes.

RHONDA   A couple of minutes? What for?

MAN	Well, I think I can work this out ... please. Just two minutes.
RHONDA	Are you a psychiatrist?
MAN	No.
RHONDA	Good. Go ahead then.
MAN	Thank you.
RHONDA	But, if he's not back inside in two minutes, my husband's coming out there.

The MAN disappears again.

	(*to SHARON*) So, Doctor Freeman, tell me, how's my son's treatment coming along?
SHARON	Now, Mrs. Penny, I am doing the best I can with Neil, but he is carrying around a lot of emotional baggage.
RHONDA	Emotional baggage? Did you hear that, Lloyd? Our son is carrying luggage around. Maybe he should be analyzed by Samsonite. Believe me, he wasn't climbing out on ledges before he started coming to you. He was normal.
LLOYD	That's right. We told him he didn't need this therapy crapola.
RHONDA	Lloyd, please, I'm talking.
LLOYD	Sorry.

The MAN on the ledge appears in the window.

MAN	Excuse, me, Sharon? Could you hand me the week-at-a-glance please?
SHARON	What?

MAN   The week-at-a-glance. Just pass it out here, would you please?

> *SHARON gets the week-at-a-glance and hands it to the MAN.*

Thank you. (*to RHONDA and LLOYD*) It's going very well, folks. Nothing to worry about. (*he disappears again, off*)

RHONDA   (*picking up the book on SHARON's desk*) Oh, will you look at this? Margaux Kenyon.

LLOYD   Oooh, pretty spicy stuff, Doctor.

SHARON   Escapism, Mr. Penny. We all need to escape once in a while.

LLOYD   Don't I know it.

RHONDA   You call yourself a psychiatrist and you read filth like this?

SHARON   You get it where you can, Lady!

RHONDA   I beg your pardon!

SHARON   I'm sorry. Look, why don't you folks have a seat? I'm sure this will all be over with very shortly. I mean, the police and the fire department are down there and Mr. Barnes has really got the gift of the gab, so I think everything is under control. (*she is near tears*)

RHONDA   Did you hear that, Lloyd? The gift of the gab is going to save our son.

LLOYD   Hell if that's all it takes, Rhonda, you could've saved him years ago.

> *LLOYD laughs. RHONDA doesn't find it amusing.*

Just trying to lighten things up.

RHONDA   Lloyd, Charlie Farquarson you're not. (*there is a scream outside*)

RHONDA   Oh, my God!

LLOYD   What the hell was that?

                      The MAN comes inside carrying his week-at-a-glance.

MAN   We've hit a bit of snag.

SHARON   What happened?

RHONDA   Where's Neil?!

MAN   He jumped.

RHONDA
& LLOYD
SHARON   (*all together*) What?!

MAN   It's okay. It's okay. He landed in the firemen's net down there.

RHONDA   Oh, Jesus, Mary and Joseph! (*she rushes to look out the window*)

LLOYD   Did he jump or did he fall?

MAN   Jumped, why?

LLOYD   Well, given his past history, I thought he might've tripped.

RHONDA   (*calling out the window*) Neil?! You stay right there! Your father and I are coming down!! And why aren't you wearing a jacket?! Come on, Lloyd.

                      RHONDA and LLOYD move to the door.

RHONDA   (*to SHARON*) And as for, you Miss Anne Bancroft in "The Miracle Worker", don't expect Neil to be coming back here again. If he wants to be depressed, we'll look after it.

                  RHONDA exits.

LLOYD   (*to SHARON*) She's not always like this. (*beat*) Actually, yes, she is.

RHONDA   (*off*) Lloyd!! (*LLOYD exits*)

MAN   So? I guess it's time to settle up, is it?

SHARON   Settle up what?

MAN   Well, we had a deal.

SHARON   Deal?

MAN   Yes, if I got him down, you'd buy a week-at-a-glance for everybody on the floor.

SHARON   I believe I said if you got him in, not down.

MAN   Hey, he's still off the ledge.

SHARON   Sorry. Now, if you don't mind, I've got a lake to get to.

                  SHARON begins packing up her briefcase.
                  ARTIE BARNES enters.

ARTIE   Doctor Freeman?

SHARON   Yes?

ARTIE   Sorry I'm late, Doctor, but the police have got the street cordoned off and the traffic is backed up for blocks.

SHARON   Late? Late for what?

ARTIE	My appointment. You told me to come at four o'clock.
SHARON	No, there must be some mistake. (*indicating the MAN*) This is my four o'clock. We're just finishing.
ARTIE	Oh.
SHARON	Are you sure I said today at four o'clock?
ARTIE	Well, pretty sure, yeah.
SHARON	And your name? (*she looks at her appointment book on the desk*)
ARTIE	Arthur Barnes. Artie.
MAN	(*moves to ARTIE and shakes his hand*) Nice to meet you, Artie. Henry Hatcher. I just stopped by to offer the doctor here a sales opportunity, but she's decided against it. Well, what'd the fella say? Some days are diamonds, some days are stones. That's the way it goes. Have we met before, Arthur? You look very familiar.
ARTIE	I don't think so.
SHARON	Mr. Barnes, I'm terribly sorry. You were right and I was wrong. Could we change your appointment to Monday at four?
ARTIE	Monday? Well, let's see. I, uh...
SHARON	Quickly now, quickly!
ARTIE	Sure, Monday would be fine.
SHARON	Good, and please accept my sincere apologies. Now, gentlemen, if you'll excuse me, I have to be somewhere.

> *SHARON finishes gathering up her things as ARTIE and the MAN talk.*

MAN   Are you sure we haven't met before, Arthur?

ARTIE   Yeah, I'm pretty sure.

MAN   Because ordinarily, I never forget a face. Can't afford to
                 in my business. You forget a client in the sales game
                 and you feel like a horse's ass. But, hey, don't get me
                 started on horses.

                        *ARTIE and SHARON exit. The MAN stands
                        there for a beat, and then it hits him.*

                 Gulliver!! Hey, get the hell back here!!

                        *The MAN exits. LLOYD enters the office, he
                        goes to the desk and picks up the Margaux
                        Kenyon book. He takes out a pen and writes
                        in the book.*

LLOYD   (*to himself as he writes*) Doctor Freeman. Here's to
                 escapism. Best wishes, Margaux Kenyon.

                        LLOYD exits. Lights down.

                        The End.